"Susan Stiffelman is knowledgeable, energetic, and can make a positive difference in your life. I highly recommend her."
--Dr. Daniel Amen, psychiatrist, author of *Change Your Brain, Change Your Life*

"Parenting Without Power Struggles is the quintessential guidebook; a must-read for parents wanting to protect their child's "authentic self," providing the much needed roadmap to navigate the calm and turbulent waters of childhood and adolescence. . . ."
-- Marilyn Mosley Gordanier, executive director of Laurel Springs School and president of the United Nations Global 500 Environmental Forum

"Raising conscious, happy, and aware children is a lofty goal. In a world that competes for our children's attention and begs them to consume, Susan Stiffelman will show you how to navigate through exceedingly difficult issues facing parents and children today and arrive successfully at the best that life can bring."
--Paul R. Scheele, co-founder of Learning Strategies Corporation, developer of ReclaimYourGenius.com

"I have been putting your advice into practice, and it is greatly contributing to my being a better father. Your book has become my "Parenting Bible" and I know I will continually refer to it. You've really created something special."
--Dr. Chris Kammer, father of four

"Susan Stiffleman's Parenting Without Power Struggles *is a breath of fresh air in a field that needs as much fresh air as it can get. Susan is well versed in a variety of disciplines that enables her to provide quality coaching, mentoring, and training for parents attempting to discover their strengths and provide the most conscious parenting possible during these very challenging times we find ourselves living in."*
--Mitch Ditkoff, co-founder and president of Idea Champions, and author of *Asleep at the Wheel*

"I just finished reading your amazing book and still have tears in my eyes. There is SO much invaluable information. I will be giving it to all my friends."
--Natasha Mellman, mother of three

Parenting Without Power Struggles *is a must-read for every parent and grandparent who wants to raise a joyful, resilient, and well-adjusted*

child. Susan Stiffelman is a marvelous human being who writes insightfully and cares immensely about the future of our children. Truly an exceptional book written with intense and compelling clarity which I will refer to often for assistance in helping not only my grandchildren but all the families we serve."
--Maria D'Angelo, founder of Children's Lifesaving Foundation

"I've known Susan Stiffelman for over twenty years, and she is absolutely wonderful. Her ability to get to the root of the problem with a child—be it emotional, academic, or psychological—makes her a treasured ally to anyone seeking long-lasting, truly positive change. I can't recommend her Parenting Without Power Struggles book highly enough!"
--Dr. Jay Gordon, pediatrician, Santa Monica

"You clearly have been given a gift of seeing into the needs of kids. . . . I also love your use of analogies and diagrams to help me grasp your concepts. Thank you from the bottom of my heart for sharing your wisdom!"
--June Louks, mother of four girls

"Susan has a way with words and showing love and compassion I have never witnessed. Although I always considered myself a good parent, Susan's approach has helped me not only deepen my relationship with my children but also help them be more of their authentic selves. Give your family the love and joy they deserve by reading Parenting Without Power Struggles."
--Susie Jill Johnson, mother of three

I have children and have worked around children (high school guidance counselor) most of my adult life. I have not seen such practical examples and "how to" guidance when dealing with our own questions of why things are not going better in our relationships. Thank you so much for putting my instincts and understandings into words. I will be recommending your book to many parents, teachers and friends.
--Mary Kay McCray, high school guidance counselor

*****

"You are a great mom, and I think a lot of people will learn and grow as parents when they read your book. Just remember, it would be nothing without me."
--Ari Andersen, Susan Stiffelman's seventeen-year-old son

Parenting Without Power Struggles

Raising Joyful, Resilient Kids While Staying Cool, Calm and *Connected*

By Susan Stiffelman, MFT

To Ari,

You have unwittingly written this book with me, teaching me

every day about how to help launch a child towards an

extraordinary life.

I love you to the moon and back, and from every corner of my

heart.

May your dreams be blessed, may *you* be blessed with joy,

peace, love, laughter, and gratitude.

And may you always feel how much you are loved.

With all my love,

Mom

Table of Contents

Introduction

Chapter 1: How to Be the Captain of the Ship Through Calm *and* Stormy Seas

Chapter 2: Attachment and Connection

Chapter 3: How to Help Your Kids Have Healthy Relationships with the Members of Their Village

Chapter 4: Creating an Unshakable Connection with Your Kids

Chapter 5: Helping Kids Deal with Frustration

Chapter 6: Handling Resistance, Anger, Whining, Meltdowns, and Aggression

Chapter 7: How to Get Kids to Cooperate

Chapter 8: Celebrate the Child You've Got

Chapter 9: Every Kid's a Genius

Chapter 10: How to Help Kids Avoid Depression and Anxiety

Chapter 11: Being Present, Mindful, and Unwinding Without Electricity

Chapter 12: Launching Children Towards a Life of True Happiness

Chapter 13: Empowering Kids to Create Their Very Best Lives

Chapter 14: Live Like Your Kids Are Watching—Because They Are

Checklists for Parents

Special Bonus Offer

Introduction

It probably comes as no surprise that my work with children and parents reflects the truth that *we teach what we most need to learn*. Like many of us growing up in the '50s and '60s (not to mention the '30s and '40s, and '70s and '80s), my parents were caring, well intentioned, and fairly clueless about how to raise kids. They did the best they could, shooting from the hip, consulting Dr. Spock, and more or less following whatever conventional parenting wisdom was available in their day and age. The result was a bit iffy.

I love my parents and thank them deeply for all they did to raise me well—which was a lot. (I mean that, Mom!) I'm also aware that if they had been provided with some basic, yet immensely useful information about child rearing, things might have been a whole lot easier for them and for their kids. In spite of the fact that I believe one can always make lemonade out of lemons, I for one wouldn't have minded growing up with slightly less dysfunction and a stronger connection to my authentic self.

I knew I wanted to work with children from the time I was a child myself, first babysitting, and then working after high school each day teaching at a day care center. I suspect my love for kids developed not only for the obvious reasons—they're cool, fun, and extremely interesting—but also because, as psychologists recognize, by healing others we can heal ourselves. As I helped children develop confidence, stand up for themselves, or learn to embrace their quirkiness, something in me was also waking up and getting stronger.

While working on getting my teaching credential, I focused on developing ways of teaching children that kept them engaged and that reawakened the excitement about learning they were born with that often had been beaten down by the time they'd reached the ripe old age of seven. In my mid-twenties I was hired as a private teacher for a family who regularly traveled around the world. With absolute freedom to customize the curriculum for each child, I understood firsthand how passionate children are to learn, when the process is creative and alive.

Eventually, I became a licensed psychotherapist, largely to add credibility to my individual work with children and teens, many who had overlapping emotional and academic issues. I seemed to attract a hefty dose of highly creative kids who were very bright but who often did poorly in school. I also found it interesting that although the majority of the children I worked with had literally everything they could possibly need from a practical and material standpoint, many suffered enormously from depression, anxiety, and a muted sense of aliveness.

One child in particular stands out in my memory to this day. James was the four-year-old younger brother of Aaron, one of the children with whom I was working. Whenever James and his mom arrived to pick up his big brother, I found myself nearly blinded by the light pouring out of him. Talk about joy! James was lit up like a Christmas tree, exuding happiness, curiosity, and exuberance for whatever life had to offer. I saw James again when he was about twelve years old, and my heart sank. He was stooped, sullen, and hardly recognizable.

I think it was at that moment that I realized I wanted to gather all that I'd come to learn as an educator, a therapist, and now a mother, and share it as best I could. The original title of this book was *Please Don't Let the Light in Your Child's Eyes Grow Dim*, and although I eventually modified it to reflect more of what I wanted the book to say, that title speaks to the origins of what you are about to read. I believe parents need to act as guardians for their children's innate light, honoring them as the emissaries of joy that they are. Instead, we often find ourselves battling over everything from homework to chores, watching as that light begins to fade.

When I took my fifteen-year-old son on a trip around the world, which included a month in Africa, I was staggered by the brightness in the eyes of nearly every child I saw. The impact of that was all the more powerful given the abject poverty and hardship surrounding them. Although I already knew in my bones that raising children to be joyful had little to do with their parents' bank accounts, the experiences I had in Africa fueled my desire to address what I believe to be the universal truths that allow parents to propel their children forward into adulthood equipped to make their lives fulfilling, joyful, and free of depression, regardless of external circumstances.

Passionate Parenting became the name of my business and website, largely because I love the word "passionate" and felt if ever there was a good use for it, it was in the realm of raising great kids. We think of passion when we talk about the way a musician approaches mastering a piece of music, or what fuels star athletes to endure grueling training sessions to be the best they can be. But why not use "passionate" to describe the feeling we parents have about wanting the best for our children?

Few of us raise our kids with apathy or indifference. Despite the fatigue, the demands, and the endless mundane tasks, there is nothing that kindles a passion in us like the desire we have to protect and care for our children. I remember being almost frightened by the intensity of the love I felt for my son when he was born; it was fierce and wild, and I was absolutely certain that if anyone tried to hurt him I would calmly break them in half. Indeed, most parents feel very passionate about parenting.

Unfortunately, although we care deeply, we often channel our emotions into controlling, combating, or giving in to our children to avoid seeing them sad, make mistakes, or experience frustration. If we really want to use the passionate feelings of love we have for our children into a healthy approach to raising them, we need to think about how we want to prepare them to most successfully live the rest of their lives.

In *Parenting Without Power Struggles: Raising Joyful, Resilient Kids While Staying Cool, Calm and Connected,* I've taken all the pieces I've collected along my own teaching, counseling, and parenting journey and assembled them into a body of information that has the power to dramatically improve your parenting life. I start with the concept of how our kids *need* us to be the captain of the ship in their lives. This isn't about parents being in control; it's about being *in charge.* You'll learn how to avoid the power struggles that once seemed inevitable when you and your child don't see eye to eye. You'll find out how to find your cool when you've temporarily lost it, regardless of whether your children are cooperating and behaving as you think they should. And you'll discover how to maintain your confidence even in the midst of those parenting storms that trigger the threats and bribes we deliver when we're feeling anything *but* powerful.

To lay the groundwork for how to be the captain of the ship in our children's lives, we'll talk about connection and attachment. When children are deeply and securely attached to us, their instincts are awakened to see us as their North Star and be receptive to our direction. We'll move on to talk about how to help kids when they're feeling frustrated, angry, and aggressive by exploring how to diffuse those intense emotions at their source. By learning how to come *alongside* your kids rather than *at* them, you'll discover you can avoid the power struggles that sometimes make interactions with your children and teens feel like dramatic courtroom battles in which each of you is arguing your case like a high-powered lawyer.

Reading on, you'll learn how to identify and nurture your children's unique gifts and talents, which for some parents may also mean coming to terms with who your child is—and is not—so you can truly accept and celebrate them as they are. Most parents have what I call their "snapshot child"—the one who says, "Sure, Mom!" the first time they're asked to take out the trash or start doing their homework. Disappointment inevitably arises when the flesh and blood child in front of you is radically different from that imaginary one. By coming to see and accept the child you *have,* emotional energy is freed up to offer the guidance and parenting he or she uniquely needs and deserves.

Later in the book you'll learn tools to help fortify your children and teens to be able to handle the problems, stressors, and challenges of life as they move towards adulthood. And finally, you're going to discover approaches that will help you empower your children to create and manifest their hopes and dreams.

Keep in mind there might be instances where I share a story about one of my clients featuring a child older than yours. These stories will help you avoid mistakes when those potential situations appear in your parenting life—usually much sooner than any of us expect!

There are many elements in *Parenting Without Power Struggles* that began to take shape decades ago, early in my teaching career. Some ideas developed later as my work with more children in a wider variety of situations helped to further shape my sensibilities. But it wasn't until I became a mother myself that this material was forged in the fires of real life. Everything you read in *Parenting Without Power Struggles* has been used as I've raised my son, who is now eighteen years old. No one has helped inspire me to grow up and be the best version of myself as my son, Ari, has. He is one cool kid. As grateful as I am for my formal education, it's raising this boy that has made everything in this book come to life.

I've made plenty of mistakes. I don't always get it right. Like you, I continue to learn and evolve on this parenthood journey. I've weathered my fair share of storms and have been knocked down more than a few times. But I have a kid who's happy, kind, and incredibly sane; and I think that has at least a little to do with the things you're going to discover as you read this book.

One day, Ari gathered up a book and a blanket and took himself out into the backyard for a good read. As he settled himself, he looked up at me, smiled, and said simply, "I love my life." That about sums up the goal of this book and of my life as a parent: to have a child who can spontaneously express something so pure and yet so simple.

I once read that when we have a child, it's as though our heart steps out of our body and starts walking around on legs of its own forevermore. The pain, the beauty, the helplessness, and the magnificence of bringing up a child are impossible and overwhelming. Sometimes, we look at our children and can hardly catch our breath. The love we feel for them brings us to our knees as we pray that they will be okay, and that their lives—today, as little ones, and onward towards what we hope will be a very long adulthood—will be blessed.

One of *my* greatest passions is helping children and parents grow into the best versions of themselves they can be. Join me on this journey, and prepare to make today the day that your parenting life gets a easier... and a lot more fun.

Chapter One
How to Be the Captain of the Ship
Through Calm *and* Stormy Seas

"A frightened captain makes a frightened crew."
Lister Sinclair

If you're a passenger on a cruise ship, it's kind of neat when the captain joins you for dinner. But his true importance isn't as a social companion; you want and need him to be the guy who oversees the smooth sailing you signed up for, steering the ship around icebergs or through storms while you blithely sing your heart out at the karaoke bar. You want to be able to depend on the captain whether or not you like him or understand everything he's doing. It's a hierarchical relationship, with the captain assuming his rightful role as the one in charge, and the passengers relaxing in the sense of safety that comes from knowing they can depend on someone competent to steer the ship through calm and rough waters.

Many parents believe it's important that their children consider them to be their friends. But in truth, children need us to be the captains of their ships. I'm not suggesting parents should be *in control* of their kids; I'm suggesting they need to be *in charge*. There's a difference. Control—as I'm using the word—is an attempt to compensate for feeling powerless or afraid. Being in charge means that we're capable of keeping our cool even when the seas are rocky—or our kids are pushing our buttons or melting down.

When our children perceive us as steady and calm—regardless of their moods or behavior—they can relax, knowing they can rely on us to get them through the challenging moments of their lives.

Imagine our reaction as passengers if we saw the captain completely lose his cool upon discovering that his vessel had a leak. Wouldn't our confidence in him take a nosedive if he ran around the deck screaming, "It can't have a leak! This is a state-of-the-art ship! We spent fifty thousand dollars getting it checked before leaving port!"

If our captain were incapable of accepting and dealing with reality, it would significantly undermine our sense of security. If he responded to a storm or an iceberg by running through the ship, shouting out in panic, "Oh no! I can't handle this!" we'd be *very* worried. In the same way, when we refuse to deal with reality as it is—our child's anger towards his sister or our teenager's use of alcohol—we leave him without the sense of comfort that comes from knowing he has someone capable of getting him safely through whatever crisis he might be experiencing.

> When our children perceive us as steady and calm—regardless of their moods or behavior—they can relax, knowing they can rely on us to get them through the challenging moments of their lives.

We all want a captain who anticipates where the rough waters might be, who adjusts his course to avoid bad weather when possible, and who stays cool when things go wrong. If there is a storm, we are far more comforted by a captain who takes charge, calling out directions to his crew with authority and issuing instructions to the passengers about where to go to be safe than we would with one who cowered in a corner or jumped ship. Similarly, when we fully inhabit the role of captain of the ship of our home and family, we set the stage for providing the quiet and comforting authority that our children so profoundly need.

A simple model to understand who, if anyone, is in charge
One of the images I use in my work is that of two hands, with the right fist representing you as the parent and the left fist representing the child. I'll be referring to this throughout the book.

In this first image, the right hand is positioned above the left. In this position we get a visual of the natural hierarchy when the parent is in charge.

Parent is in charge

This image represents you as captain of the ship. You're calm and confident, and you exude the quiet authority that comes from being certain that you can navigate the ship through calm and stormy seas.

When the hands are side by side, no one is in charge. I call this "The Two Lawyers." This is where power struggles take place, with each side debating the merits of their position, and the one most committed—or least exhausted—prevails.

No one is in charge: "The Two Lawyers"

And when the left hand, representing the child, is above the right hand, the child is essentially in charge. The parent feels powerless, and resorts to bribes, threats or overpowering the child to in an attempt to exert control.

Child is in charge

I'll be expanding on this idea throughout the book, but here's a simple scenario that will lay the groundwork for understanding it:

Your daughter asks if she can have a sleepover, and you kindly but confidently say, "I'm afraid tonight's not a good night for that." This image would apply:

Parent is in charge

Let's say your daughter asks, "Why can't I?" and you reply, "Because you're obviously too tired. You've been crabby since you got home from soccer." Your daughter says, "No, I'm not; I just had a bad game," and you respond with, "I don't think it's because you had a bad game, honey. You were cranky before you left the house." And your daughter says, "I was only cranky because you were trying to make me eat cereal I hate." And you say, "You usually love that cereal!" And she says . . . —you get the picture. You're now in the land of "The Two Lawyers."

No one is in charge: "The Two Lawyers"

If the situation deteriorates further still, you'll hear your daughter say something like, "If you don't let me have a sleepover, I'm not going to take out the trash." You respond, "Oh yes, you most certainly are, young lady, if you want to watch any TV for the rest of the weekend!" (Note the desperate tone creeping into your voice as you attempt to assert your authority.) For all practical purposes, the child is now running the show, and you're issuing either threats or bribes to try to get back in charge.

Child is in charge

I'll be elaborating on this further, but hopefully this gives you a sense of the differences between being truly in charge, jockeying for the role of ship captain with your child, and trying to overpower her into giving you that position back when things have deteriorated.

The following is a real-life example to illustrate how easily this can happen between parent and child.

The challenge of getting a sleepy, unmotivated eleven-year old up for school in the morning

Stella came to me in utter frustration. Her eleven-year-old son, Sam, refused to get up for school and every morning was so filled with drama that both mother and son were emotionally drained before they had even begun their day. Stella reported that every morning she went into Sam's room and woke him up sweetly with a kind voice and a little foot rub.

No response. Stella then said she would speak just a little more loudly and grab those feet just a bit more firmly. Sam would emit groans and moans. At this point Stella would begin to get a little impatient. "Honey, remember we talked about this last night, and you agreed to get up on time today?" Silence. "Okay, Sam, I'm warning you. I'm going to go get your brother ready and put breakfast on the table. If you don't get up in one minute, you're gonna be late!"

It's important to understand that Sam doesn't actually have a problem. Either he doesn't care if he's late or he doesn't yet have access to the part of his brain that believes getting to school on time matters. Promises made the night before are filed in some part of his memory that is so distant they might as well be stored on another planet. So far, the only one with a dilemma is Mom, and she's starting to panic because she's having trouble forcing Sam to solve her problem.

So now what happens? Mom ends up going into Sam's room five more times, yelling, threatening to leave without him, and lecturing him about why "this simply cannot and will not happen again" (something she says every morning, suggesting she has very little credibility in her son's eyes.) Stella has totally lost her cool despite vowing to keep it together, and she's angry with herself—and Sam—for being unable to avoid this train wreck yet again.

Sam, scrambling to get dressed, matches his mother's drama with his own, screaming about how Mom should've woken him a different way, or maybe blaming his brother, whose coughing in the night woke him up and made him especially tired. Sam has little awareness—despite Mom's valiant efforts to enlighten him—that every morning he has a list of excuses.

No one is in charge: "The Two Lawyers"

The family rushes out the door, tense, stressed, and either yelling at one another or hardly speaking. Stella tells her son that it's his fault that she got angry. Mom comes home from the school drop-off feeling remorseful, angry, and powerless to see a way out of this daily morning chaos.

Child is in charge

When your child doesn't do what you ask and you become emotional or begin issuing ever-escalating threats, he senses your panic. Your dramatic responses literally shift the hierarchy; for all practical purposes, you've handed responsibility for the outcome over to the child. This is not being the captain of your ship!

Pushing creates power struggles and resistance

In my workshops, I illustrate an important idea by having a participant stand up with their palms against mine. Without giving any instructions, I lean forward, pushing forcibly against their hands. Invariably, they push back with equal or greater force. After this demonstration I ask, "Did I ask you to push against me?" Their answer is always, "No, actually, you didn't!"

What we discover is that when one person in a relationship starts pushing, the other *instinctively* pushes back. But you can't have two people pushing against each other if one of them doesn't participate. You can't have a power struggle with only one person engaged.

You can't have a power struggle with only one person

Although the actual words and actions you take with a child who won't get up in the morning will depend on all kinds of variables—his investment in getting to school on time, his age, the consequences he might face from teachers if he's late—what's important is the energetic place you inhabit as you parent. When you're firmly rooted in your authority as the captain of the ship, these dramatic, escalating interactions with your children cannot happen. The captain doesn't negotiate with his crew or passengers to be in charge; he simply *is* in charge.

What is the first requirement for staying grounded in your authority? Remain calm, at all costs. It becomes much easier to stay centered when you let go of giving your children the power to make or break your serenity depending on how they behave.

Back to Stella

I asked Stella this question: "What importance have you assigned to your child getting to school on time? Do you worry about receiving a call from a judgmental office lady announcing that your son will be staying after school because he has too many tardies? Have you decided that it's the mark of a 'good mother' to instill a sense of responsibility in you child? Have you interpreted his nonchalant attitude about being late to school as meaning you have failed to teach him the importance of punctuality? *What are you making your son's behavior mean?"*

When we give our children the power to make us feel that we are or aren't good parents—or good people—we've relegated the job of steering the ship to them, all the while hoping, threatening, and begging them to guide it in the particular way we want it to go so we get the outcome we think we need.

I helped Stella use a process that relates to this issue: *The Work*[1] by Byron Katie. Katie's approach is based on the understanding that it's not the events around us that trigger our upset but rather our thoughts and beliefs about those events. In the context of parenting, it's our beliefs and stories about how our kids should behave that cause us to lose our cool. For some of us, we know we're stuck in a story of our own creation if our heart starts pounding and our mind starts obsessively replaying what they did. For others, we find ourselves tempted to tell our friends about our child's misbehavior to get validation for our anger. And many parents deliver unproductive, or even irrational threats to get their kids to listen and obey. The Work is about looking at these beliefs and reactions so we can be free of their negative influence on how we respond to the challenges of parenting.

> It's not the events around us that trigger our upset but rather our thoughts and beliefs *about* those events. It's our stories about how our kids *should* behave that cause us to lose our cool.

The Work consists of asking four questions about the belief or thought that precipitates our upset.

The four questions:
1. Is it true?
2. Can you absolutely know that it's true?
3. How do you feel (or react) when you think that thought?
4. Who would you be without that thought?

One way to identify the thought at the core of our upset is to find a statement with the word "should" or "shouldn't" in it, and to then determine whether or not that thought causes you to feel a strong rush of negative emotion. Look for a belief that gets your blood boiling and sends adrenalin coursing through your veins—one that has some juice behind it, or that gets you to go from zero to sixty in a few seconds. Typically, it will be a thought that prompts you to start building a case, like a lawyer, and to then look for evidence that justifies your strong reaction. Some examples:

> *"My kids should come to dinner the first time I call them."*
> *"My husband shouldn't give our son junk food when I'm not home."*
> *"My son should take a shower."*
> *"My daughter shouldn't whine."*

These kinds of thoughts throw us off our game and cause us to lose that calm feeling of being in charge. They also prompt us to come *at* our kids—provoking their defensiveness and resistance—rather than coming *alongside* them, which promotes their receptivity.

Using the four questions with Stella

Here is how I used this approach with Stella. First, we identified the upsetting belief that set in motion her ineffective way of dealing with the morning drama with her son:

"My son, Sam, should try to get up for school on time in the morning."

I asked Stella, "Is it true that your son should try to get up for school on time?"

Stella responded, "Of course it's true. It's important for Sam to learn how to manage his time and work within schedules. And it gets his day off to a better start when he's not frantically scrambling into the classroom door at the last minute."

I responded, "Okay, I understand. Getting up late creates problems. Now, can you absolutely know that it's true that your son should try up on time for school in the morning?"

Sounding a little hesitant, but still defensive, Stella replied,

"Well, I can't absolutely know it's true. I *wish* he would wake up on time to get to school, but I can't *absolutely* know that it's true that he should. The reality is that he certainly doesn't *want* to get up on time."

I probed a little further with the third question. "How do you react or behave when you believe this story that Sam should try to get up on time for school in the morning, and he doesn't?"

"I'm tense, frustrated, and upset with him for creating this drama every day. I judge him: 'Why can't he be more responsible? Why is he so lazy? Why is he doing this to me?' I don't feel any of those warm, fuzzy mommy feelings when I think about all this. I take it personally, seeing his behavior as a sign of disrespect towards his teacher and towards me. I feel helpless, and I'm angry with him for making me feel that way."

"Stella, here's the fourth question: Who would you be without this thought, this story that your son should try to get up on time in the morning? How would you be different if you simply noticed that he wasn't getting ready, without the negative commentary running in your mind? Now remember, I'm not asking you to stop caring about getting him to school on time, or to abandon all hope of helping him learn how to get himself up in the morning. I'm just asking who you'd be if you didn't feel the tension and frustration that come from believing this story so staunchly?"

She thought for a moment and said, "Well, if I didn't believe he should try to get up on time, I suppose I'd be much more relaxed about the whole thing. I might be curious about what would happen if I didn't push and pull him. Now that I think about it, maybe if I were less attached to him getting up on time, he might compensate for my lack of anxiety about it by coming up with some strategies of his own for moving the morning along better."

"Okay, that's great, Stella. Now let's look at the turnaround. Can we look at how the opposite of 'My son should get up on time for school' might be true? Give me three reasons that there might be some truth or value in 'My son *shouldn't* get up on time in the morning for school.' Or that *it makes sense—in its own way*-- that he doesn't try to get up on time for school."

"Whoa. That sounds like I'm signing up to be a bad parent. All right, I'll give it a go. One reason? He doesn't like school and puts it off as long as possible. He loves the feeling of being cozy in bed and wants to enjoy it as long as he can. He is, after all, a kid, and most kids would rather be home in their comfy bed than in a 'boring' classroom."

Stella paused and then said, "Second reason? It could be that he's really tired. Sam has trouble falling asleep at night, and I've often wondered whether he's actually getting enough rest. He does seem genuinely sleepy in the morning when I wake him.

And maybe a third reason is that he's been struggling a lot with his schoolwork. He even told me last week that he thinks he's stupid. So I guess maybe he's not all that motivated to go to a place where he doesn't feel very confident or successful.

Wow! I can't believe I could actually come up with three reasons why his behavior makes its own kind of sense. Now that I'm thinking this way, I can actually think of other reasons he might not be motivated to roll out of bed when I want him to!"

Stella came to understand that if she loosened her grip on the story of what her son should be doing, and considered the possibility that there might be reasons for Sam's slow-motion morning behavior, she might be better able to approach the situation in a healthy way. More importantly, until she stopped making Sam's behavior responsible for her anger and frustration, she would continue to engage in this power struggle with her son. I told Stella, "He who is most attached to a particular outcome has the least amount of power."

When we become willing to take a hard look at the beliefs and stories we maintain—often while we're busily gathering all kinds of evidence to support their validity—we become capable of dealing with our kids in a way that promotes their receptivity rather than their resistance. Taking an honest look at our judgments about their behaviors allows us to have conversations with our kids that don't come with the aroma of needing them to be different so *we* can feel better.

If you want children to be receptive to you, clean up what's going on between your ears—the thoughts and stories that precipitate your anger, fear, or disappointment—before you try to have any influence over them. Difficult conversations go far better without the negative stories and judgments that affect how you conduct yourself.

By the way, this process is equally valuable with spouses, bosses, and neighbors. Imagine how much better a conversation with your chronically late husband might be if you first dealt with the thought "John shouldn't leave things for the last minute" and instead discovered a few reasons why he *should* leave things for the last minute. "He feels more focused doing things at the last minute. He gets a lot done in a short amount of time. He has a prefrontal cortex that requires adrenalin to kick-start his energy when the things he has to do are boring." Having done this mental exercise, you would then be able to ask for help in managing the anxiety *you* feel when he's rushing around at the last minute as the two of you are trying to leave the house without the blame, shame, and guilt trips that make him feel judged and cause him to resist and slow down.

Consider whether what you're saying opens or closes the door to the other person you want to influence. Does being under the influence of your negative beliefs help or hurt in getting your message across? Most likely it sabotages your goal of resolving a problem by transforming what could be useful discussion into a power struggle.

> Consider whether what you're saying opens or closes the door to the other person you want to influence.

Thoughts as drugs

I think in images and have created one that often helps my clients better understand the effects their beliefs have on their behavior and experience. I explained to Stella the idea of thoughts as drugs.

"Imagine we took that upsetting thought of yours—'Sam should try to get up on time for school in the morning'—and compressed it into pill form. Now, as with any pill or drug, when you swallow that pill, you're under the influence of the drug that it contains, which in this case is the influence of that belief. That story you've chosen to believe infiltrates your consciousness, and you're now at the mercy of its effect on you."

Stella liked this analogy and gave a half smile as she said, "Well, I can think of a whole lot of 'pills' I swallow when it comes to my kids—and my husband!"

"Okay, now about Sam's not getting up in time: try to imagine *not* swallowing that pill. Imagine *not* being under the influence of that belief—not having it take hold of you. How might you be different around Sam if you didn't so firmly believe that he should try to get up for school on time? And how might he receive your input if you weren't so staunchly defending your belief about his behavior?"

"I imagine he'd be far more open to me if I were more relaxed and didn't come at him so aggressively."

Stepping back to look at the situation objectively, Stella was able to get clear about what she was making Sam's behavior mean. The first thing she realized was that she was making it something he was doing personally to her. Naturally, when she believed Sam's slow motion movements were intended to deliberately show his mom that he didn't respect her, it triggered her anger. When I guided Stella through the four questions around the belief, "Sam doesn't try to wake up on time in the morning because he doesn't respect me" she quickly became clear that it wasn't true.

She looked at the many ways her son *did* respect her, and realized that his problems waking up had far more to do with his fatigue or disinterest in school than it did with wanting to make trouble for her.

Another belief Stella discovered that had been fueling her anger had to do with what she believed other people thought about her when she repeatedly pulled up late at school to drop Sam off, just as the final bell was ringing. She admitted she didn't want to look bad in the eyes of other parents and the office staff.

As she became willing to see how she had been misinterpreting her son's motives, or how she was trying to use his behavior to gain the approval of others, Stella became more empowered to consider ways to activate Sam's internal motivation to get to school on time in a way that was "clean."

Soon after our meeting, Stella went into Sam's room in the early evening and invited him to have a talk. The two of them had shared some laughs earlier at the dinner table. As the captain of the ship, Stella noticed that the waters were calm and that this might be a good time for a little "maintenance." Sam was open to talking, and Stella began by setting the tone as being between allies rather than adversaries.

"Sweetie, I've been thinking about our mornings—taking a good look at what goes on that creates all the stress." Sam became defensive, assuming his mom was about to lay into him as usual: "Mom, it's not my fault! My alarm clock always seems to break, and a lot of times you don't help by getting all uptight and mean!"

Having done her work in advance, Stella didn't start defending herself. She also didn't try to take apart her son's excuses, as she would have done in the past.

Parent is in charge

"Honey, I know it's hard for you to get up in the morning. I get that. I imagine it's not easy to pop out of bed early in the morning when you're tired and want to sleep some more. It must be hard when you're feeling so cozy. Especially when I get so upset." Sam seemed taken aback by what his mom was saying. "What's it like for you, Sam, to have to get up so early every day?"

"It sucks."

Stella responded gently. "I see that, honey. The more I think about it, the more I picture how hard it might be to hear that alarm in the morning. I can imagine you'd much rather roll over and go back to sleep. I wonder if it's even harder lately, now that it seems like your schoolwork has gotten more difficult." Mom knew she may not be offering the right reasons, but she wanted her son to get the feeling that she truly wanted to understand the situation from Sam's vantage point.

"Yea, it is hard. I just hate getting up. It's so stupid that school starts so early."

"Sam, wouldn't it be fantastic if schools could be redesigned to start at ten in the morning!"

"Yes! Or, like, noon!"

"And I'll bet it would be easier to get up for school if you knew all the work would be easy. That would be the perfect fantasy school: One that started at noon and just had easy schoolwork to do!"

Sam chimed in, "Yea! And NO MATH AT ALL!"

By creating a loving atmosphere and giving her son the feeling that she was on his side, Stella was helping him feel receptive to her suggestions and support. He ended up telling her more about his struggles with Math, and Stella began to brainstorm ways to help him get back on track with that subject. She was being the calm, confident captain of the ship that her son needed, rather than a frantic mom who was desperate to change his behavior so *she* could feel okay.

From this place of *genuine* authority, Stella moved the conversation towards some solutions to their morning drama. Together they came up with some new ideas. Sam agreed to get his backpack in the car by 9:00 pm. the night before. Stella offered to wake him up with a protein smoothie that gave him a little boost and helped him feel more alert and grounded. They agreed it would be better for her to wake him ten minutes earlier so Sam could linger in bed a little while. As Stella practiced holding her position as captain of the ship and keeping the turmoil out of their morning routine, she was amazed at how much more willing Sam was to try his best to wake up on time.

One day, after Sam had been getting himself up and out the door successfully for a few weeks, Stella took the boys to school as usual. After her younger son darted out of the car on his way to class, Stella caught Sam's hand and said, "Close the door, sweetie." To her son's astonishment and delight, today was going to be a Hooky Day for just the two of them. Stella drove out to a nearby lake and pulled out a bag of things she'd secretly packed the night before: comic books (Sam's favorites), checkers, and some art supplies. The two of them shared a wonderful day together, munching on the picnic lunch Stella had packed, and reconnecting.

Stella noticed that the mornings went even better after that, although she also came to understand that her son most likely was simply not a morning person and that he might continue to struggle with getting himself out the door on time. But with his Mom as the captain of the ship, rather than a fellow passenger who needed him to behave a certain way so she could feel okay, their ship resumed smoother sailing.

Using the image of your two hands to understand the parent-child dynamic

When Stella participated in dramatic, heated discussions and negotiations with her son, each fighting over the merits of what the other had to say, she was participating in "The Two Lawyers," in which parent and child each attempt to build the strongest case in order to "win." Parents who engage in these kinds of angry negotiations and battles are forfeiting their role as captain of the ship.

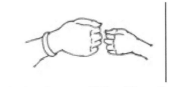

No one is in charge: "The Two Lawyers"

When Stella suggested to Sam that it was Sam's fault that Stella had gotten angry, she was making her son responsible for her ability—or inability—to keep her cool and be in charge.

When parents convince themselves that their children *make* them upset or force them to resort to threats or bribes, the children are in charge. Passengers are not meant to be captains; when they attempt to take over the leadership position, problems are inevitable.

Child is in charge

When Stella came *alongside* her son, acknowledging his point of view without pushing against him or creating a power struggle, she positioned herself to be calm and confident, evoking his receptivity. When a ship captain knows he's in charge, he doesn't flaunt it or need to convince the passengers; nor does he need them to like him. He owns his role, with or without their approval.

Parent is in charge

Children want and need to feel dependent on us
As fun as a passenger might think it would be if the captain were to hand the steering wheel over to him, after a moment or two she would start to feel edgy and begin insisting that the skipper take over. As passengers, we want the sense of security that comes from knowing the captain is confidently at the helm.

Have you ever noticed the difference in children's behavior when there's a blackout or a disaster, or when they're in a foreign country? Kids are more compliant and cooperative when they're in an unfamiliar situation; their natural instincts to follow their parents are fully activated in these situations. There's something about being dependent on a parent that's comforting to a child. (I've even seen parents who've tripped the circuit breakers in their house when things got terribly out of hand in order to "create" a blackout situation in which the kids had to look to mom and dad for guidance and comfort!) Children want us to be lovingly in charge. They need it.

There are hundreds of situations in which parents forfeit their position as captain, but I've yet to see one that couldn't be corrected by these approaches:

> Focus on loosening your need for your child to behave properly so that you can feel you're a good parent.
>
> Explore the meaning you're assigning to your child's problematic behavior.
>
> Let go of the drama and threats that simply emphasize how out of control you've become.
>
> Come *alongside* your child, rather than *at* him, so he feels you're his ally and advocate.
>
> Create a plan and stick to it with quiet authority, even at the cost of having your child dislike you.
>
> Love your child in the way he most needs it: by being the calm, confident captain of the ship as your child navigates the sometimes smooth, sometimes rough, waters of growing up.

Questions and Suggestions

Question: *How can I tell the difference between a threat and a consequence?*

Suggestion: Simple. A threat is delivered by someone who feels angry, frustrated, and/or out of control. It's delivered with hostility, desperation, and aggression. The child is in charge.

Child is in charge

A consequence is presented with compassion by a parent who inhabits the role as captain of the ship. It sounds and feels clean, caring, and calm. It's delivered without a lot of extra words and has a tone of quiet authority.

Parent is in charge

***

Question: *As my seven-year-old son got out of the car this morning, he punched his five-year-old brother in the face for calling him "Stupid." I freaked out. As much as I like what you say about being cool and in charge, if anyone—including my other offspring—deliberately injures one of my children, the mother lion in me wakes up and roars. I was furious, and as far from calm as possible. What could I have done differently?*

Suggestion: This is one of those examples where the apparent problem—your son punching his younger brother—can distract you from recognizing the real problem. While there are inevitably times when raw immaturity causes a child to act on impulse, many of the upsetting things our children do are symptoms of a different issue. I would start by encouraging you to comfort your injured son, saying little to the older boy while mothering the younger one as needed.

Next, I would ask you to shift your focus from what to do *after* the fight happened, to the events leading up to that moment. How did the morning go? Did your boys get enough sleep, or were they up late the night before? Did they have waffles and sugary syrup or a balanced, protein-rich breakfast? Do you feel you and your older son are close these days, or does he often show signs of being out of synch and disconnected from you? Was the punch a surprise, or does it seem as though he's continually walking around with a low-grade "fever" of frustration, anger, or sadness? Does your son like to go to school and look forward to it, or does he dread it? What's the relationship like between the two boys? Is there a lot of competitiveness and jockeying for position, or do they generally get along well? If there's a lot of ongoing tension between them, can you see the root of it? Have you considered ways to create more of a natural bond between them rather than offering lectures about how they *should* love each other and get along?

Ship captains don't just deal with problems when they appear; they scan the horizon for icebergs or storms so they can avoid them. I'm more interested in helping parents *prevent* outbursts than trying to find the right thing to say or do after they occur. Since you are the captain of the ship for your child, you have the opportunity to orchestrate his day to help create the greatest likelihood that he will be successful. Instead of looking for Band-Aid solutions—like figuring out what to do when your older son hits his younger brother—I would encourage you to consider how to prevent this from happening.

I would suggest that you take a look at a number of things, many of which I elaborate on in later chapters:

Make sure your kids are getting good food and plenty of sleep. We're all pretty nasty when we're hungry, tired, and going somewhere we don't want to go.

Work to reconnect with your older son if your attachment with him seems fragile or weak. And take steps to fortify a real connection between your two sons. (See chapter 2.)

Gently approach your son when he expresses frustration about school, his younger brother, or whatever seems to chronically bug him. He may need to offload a buildup of general frustration that leaks out when the slightest thing offends him. (See chapter 5.)

Teach him ways to describe his feelings and look at the ways his thoughts fuel his anger. Help translate and put into words what he's feeling. (See chapter 6.)

Manage your own distress so you can be the calm, clear-headed parent he needs when he's hurt, angry, or frustrated. You offer him his best shot at learning how to manage his own reactions when he sees you staying centered, even in the midst of the storm.

Take an honest look at the opposite of whatever thoughts get you so triggered that you lose your temper. This might be as simple as transforming the phrase "My son shouldn't hit his little brother" into "My son *should* hit his little brother." If you, as captain of the ship, are willing to consider that if your older boy is hungry, tired, disconnected from you, chronically frustrated, sick of going to school, or secretly thinking he is stupid, then you may be able to see why hitting his brother is an inevitable response to being teased. By keeping your cool and helping your son feel his feelings fully, you can guide him from frustration to adaptation.

Meanwhile, after the incident has happened (although I hope it won't happen as frequently once some of these ideas are implemented), calmly approach your children and say something like, "You boys are clearly having a rough morning. We're going to need to do things differently; hitting and mean words aren't allowed." In a quiet voice you may tell both boys the consequence of their choices, but your goal for the moment is first to simply help all of you settle down.

In my way of thinking, a "clean" consequence is the natural result of a choice a child has made, based simply on the notion of cause and effect. Rather than invent random consequences in the heat of the moment (better known as simply punishments in disguise), I prefer that parents tell their children *in advance* what sorts of things will happen if they make a poor decision, or if they cross lines, like hitting or insulting. For some families, this might mean doing something practical: If Shane deliberately breaks Ethan's toy, he will need to earn some or all of the money to replace it. For others, it might mean making emotional amends: If Shane chooses to hurt his brother by breaking his toy, he needs to do something helpful for Ethan, such as spend a half an hour helping him work on his science project.

My favorite format for introducing consequences to children is in a family meeting: Children take this even more seriously if you have a clipboard and take notes while the family discusses possible outcomes for failing to live up to the family's standards of cooperation and kindness. (As an aside, I am not a big fan of forcing children to apologize, and then assuming things are back on track. While this is sometimes all that's necessary, children who chronically violate others and are coerced into offering up an apology simply become good at apologizing; they don't generally modify their behavior very much.)

There may be times when your child has misbehaved and you will spontaneously announce that he's going to have to do extra chores or forego playing with a friend. Still, my preference is that parents prevent problems rather than focus on what to do after they've occurred.

While a ship captain might steer northwest if that's the direction of his final destination, if he's in the midst of a storm and traveling northwest means he's going to be pummeled by waves, he's going to temporarily head southeast. Similarly, during the storm of your child's misbehavior, avoid lecturing, explaining, or advising. This is not a teachable moment. First, get through the storm, and then talk about how you got there, after you've all settled down.

Resist the temptation to focus exclusively on this incident; look at the bigger picture of what was fueling your son's aggressiveness. If you see this morning's problem in a larger context, chances are you'll be able to change what fueled the problem, so you can avoid a repeat performance in the future.

Question: *I've tried all kinds of things to keep from yelling at my kids. Even though I like your ideas—and I admit I haven't used your approach yet—I have tried a lot of things like counting to ten and trying to remember how much I love my kids when I'm struggling to not lose my temper, all without much success. Do you really believe somebody like me, who's so naturally fiery and reactive, can learn to be calm when I've developed so many bad habits?*

Suggestion: Yes! One of the things that most compelled me to write this book was the feedback from people like you who reported that these approaches really did help them to stop the blood-boiling reactivity that caused them to yell at their kids. We all come with unique temperaments, and some of us tend to run "hotter" than others. But it's always our thoughts about the events of our lives—rather than the events themselves—that cause us to be upset. A person with a shorter fuse rushes more quickly from zero to sixty, but the precipitator that ignites his fuse is still going to be the meaning he assigns to whatever triggers his reaction.

If you try the various strategies for stepping back from the thoughts and beliefs that kick you into the mire of frustration and anger, including the Four Questions as presented in this chapter, it will no longer be so easy for you to get thrown off by your children's behavior. (You may also want to sign up for my Parenting Without Power Struggles newsletter at www.passionateparenting.net to help you maintain support for instituting these new approaches.)

Rather than asking you to "just think positive thoughts" or to vent about your frustration, I invite you to challenge the beliefs and stories that cause you to lose your temper. Doing so will help you dissipate anger at its source. I'm excited for you to try these approaches; and I'm confident that if you do, you're going to find yourself no longer willing to be yanked around by the stories that bring on those bouts of shouts. It feels good to parent from a place of quiet authority. And yes, doing so is within your reach.

To recap, the Four Questions are:

1. Is it true?

2. Can you absolutely know that it's true?

3. How do you feel (or react) when you think that thought?

4. Who would you be without that thought?

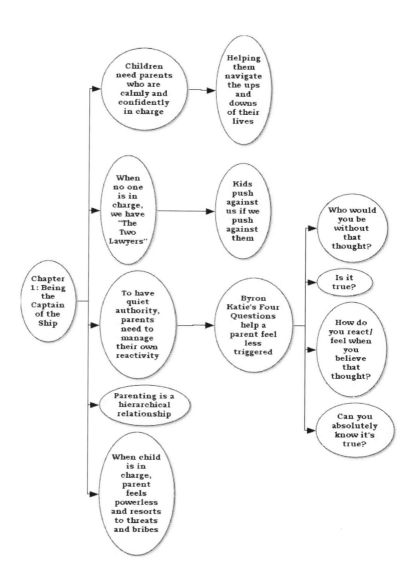

Chapter Two
Attachment and Connection

"Empathy, caring, sharing, inhibition of aggression, capacity to love and a host of other characteristics of a healthy, happy and productive person are related to the core attachment capabilities which are formed in infancy and early childhood."
Dr. Bruce Perry[1]

Summarizing the results of a two-year study of twelve thousand teenagers[2], gender researchers Cate and Dooley[3] wrote, "Researchers discovered that the best predictor of a teenager's health and the strongest deterrent to high-risk behavior was a close relationship with a parent. They concluded that a strong emotional connection with at least one parent or significant adult figure reduces the odds that an adolescent will suffer from emotional stress, have suicidal thoughts or behavior, engage in violence, or use substances (tobacco, alcohol or marijuana). Good relationships help create resilience to dangerous, acting-out behavior in our children."

The greatest insurance policy parents can "buy" to ensure their children will grow up to be healthy and resilient is to forge and maintain strong emotional connections. The bonds of deep attachment begin to form when children are little. While some parents may find it relatively easy to build connection with an easy or younger child, it's vital that if the parent-child relationship begins to break down, they recognize and take steps to regain that all-important connection.

Robert's daughter starts drifting away
Recently, I received a call from a father who was concerned about his teenage daughter. Robert began the conversation by saying, "When Rosie was born, I was flooded with love and with the feeling that there wasn't a thing in the world I wouldn't do for her. As she got a little older, we formed our own mutual admiration society; I could do no wrong in her eyes, and she was

the jewel of my heart. During her grade school years, we were so connected that I was sure nothing could come between us. Rosie's mother passed away when Rosie was three, so we were especially close. She told me everything—all of her frustrations and worries, and problems with friends and teachers. As she headed toward her teen years, she hit a few bumps in the road as she found herself missing and needing her mother in a new way, but we got through it. In fact, sometimes I'd listen to friends talk about challenges with their kids her age, and I'd secretly think that they were doing something wrong, because I wasn't having *any* of their issues.

"Well, fast-forward to the last six months. Rosie was spending much more time with her friends than with me. I figured that was pretty normal, so I tried not to worry about it; I thought it was just part of the natural separation from parents that all teens go through. Around the time of her fifteenth birthday it seemed like she was moody all the time. I chalked it up to adolescence and hormones and all that, although I have to admit there was a part of me that was worried.

"Lately she's gotten more withdrawn, to the point where she hardly talks to me about anything. Friends with daughters Rosie's age told me her behavior was normal, and I knew it had to be hard because she's becoming a young lady and doesn't have a mom. But I had a lot of mixed feelings about whether I should do something or let things be. I guess I was in denial about the fact that Rosie might be steering off course. I couldn't believe that *my* daughter, the sunshine of my life and the little girl who was so incredibly close to me, might drift away. But the truth is, I hardly know her, and I had to finally admit that.

The clincher happened last night when the mother of one of Rosie's friends sent me an email with her Facebook link. When I looked at it, I crumbled. The bizarre things she says she's interested in, the lies she tells about herself, the depression she describes, and the provocative pictures she had for everyone to see . . ."

Robert's voice trailed off; he couldn't finish the story for a while, but I knew it well because I hear it often. The attachment between this father and his daughter—once seemingly indestructible—had become too weak to sustain his connection to her.

The Six Stages of Attachment

Psychologist Gordon Neufeld[4] has created an excellent model for understanding the way healthy relationships develop. He presents *six stages of attachment* that create the foundation for virtually every relationship your child will ever have, beginning with Mommy and Daddy, and later with siblings, friends, and intimate partners.

Attachment is the most primal need of the child, surpassing even hunger in its importance. All effective efforts to shape a child's behavior originate from safe and secure attachment. Think of it as the cornerstone of every aspect of parenting, including managing challenging behavior, keeping kids on track academically, and maintaining the all-important role of being the one they turn to for advice and support.

> Attachment is the most primal need of the child, surpassing even hunger in its importance.

Attachment makes parenting easy. It awakens a child's natural desire to please us, follow our lead, and be receptive to our guidance. Within the context of close connection, our children like our company and feel at home with us. In the same way that we tolerate the stinkiness of our own baby's dirty diaper but have to hold our nose when we change someone else's, attachment endears our children to us. (When you're "out of attachment" to someone—including your young child or your teen—you may even find that their breath is more offensive to you than when you're lovingly connected!) What follows is a brief overview of the six phases of attachment, after which I'll go into each one in more depth.

The most primitive and basic stage of attachment is **Proximity**. Through touch, contact, and closeness, the infant begins the journey of attaching to her mother and father. At around the age of two, the attachment goes deeper as the toddler seeks **Sameness** with her parents, mimicking their mannerisms or dress, and looking for ways to be the same as Mommy or Daddy. The next stage is **Belonging** or **Loyalty**. In this stage we'll see the three-year-old possessively refer to "**My** mommy!" Four-year-old children look for reassurance of the durability of their attachment to their parents by seeking evidence of their **Significance**, understanding that Mommy and Daddy (or whoever the caregiver might be) will hold close that which is special or precious to them. Around the age of five we see the beginnings of genuine **Love** as attachment goes ever deeper. And finally, from age six onward, if the attachment roots have gone deeply enough, we have a child who allows herself to venture out into **Being Known**.

All relationships will follow these six stages: *Proximity, Sameness, Belonging/Loyalty, Significance, Love, and Being Known*. Each stage solidifies the attachment between parent and child. Conversely, if any of these areas is weak (e.g., if the child doesn't feel special to you, or if the child doesn't feel your loyalty to her), then the relationship itself will weaken. (For more information, please take a look at *Hold On to Your Kids* by Gordon Neufeld.)

***

Let's go into these in a bit more detail.

Proximity

When you invite a child to be in your company, you're promoting Proximity. This most basic invitation to be close to your child—whether it's cuddling, snuggling, or playing a game of chess—tells him that you want to be connected. When this message is compromised—when you clearly *don't* want to be around your child (perhaps because his behavior has been off-putting or because he has misbehaved)—you threaten his most fundamental need: to be securely attached to you.

If a child does not have the sense that their parents find pleasure in their company, they move toward becoming peer- rather than parentally-attached, taking their cues from their friends. They obsessively seek Proximity with their buddies, following *their* lead while rejecting your input or guidance. Parents often promote peer bonding because we think it's a natural part of growing up. We need to be aware of the danger of opting out of closeness with our children simply because they now prefer to be with their social group.

While I have nothing against kids preferring their friends' company as they get older, I believe it is *not* in our youngsters' best interests to allow our connection with them to wither simply because they don't find us cool anymore. Throughout childhood *and adolescence*, children need parents who remain committed to being trusted advisors and stewards as they grow up.

Sameness

When you and your child have something in common, whether it's a fondness for horseback riding, watching the Lakers, or eating Rocky Road ice cream, you're strengthening your attachment through Sameness. By emphasizing things you both enjoy doing or are interested in, you fuel the connection between the two of you. When you have a child whose interests are distinctly different from your own—for whatever reason—it's important that you find something your child cares about that you can relate to.

A child who feels he has nothing in common with his parents will either feel terribly lonely or will seek Sameness with his peers. (And he will often still feel lonely, because peers are so terribly fickle in their attachments.) The twelve- or fourteen-year-old girl who dresses, talks, and behaves just like her friends is seeking attachment with them through Sameness. We chalk this up as typical behavior for teens and move ourselves out of the picture, when instead we need to find ways to reinforce a sense of similarity, in one way or another, with our children.

Rosie had sent her father the message that she had no interest in spending time with him, focusing instead on hanging out with her friends or being alone in her room. Robert realized that he had accepted her withdrawal, buying into the notion that teenagers have nothing in common with their parents. Ignoring his instincts, he had come to accept it as normal that Rosie would dress, talk, and think like her peers, while gradually shutting out her father more and more.

Belonging or Loyalty

The third stage of attachment, Belonging or Loyalty, strengthens attachment by emphasizing to the child that you are unequivocally his champion and on his side. When you stand up for a child, when you "have his back," so to speak, you're reinforcing his need to know that he can lean on you. One of the most painful experiences for a child who is not securely attached is when he perceives his parent as his adversary rather than his ally, as when Mom takes the side of the teacher when there's a problem at school, or when Dad—who's also his son's soccer coach—reprimands him for a bad play in front of all the other kids.

When attachment via Belonging/Loyalty goes awry, children retreat by becoming angry, aggressive, or withdrawn or—as is very common—by focusing their loyalties on their peers. The problem with children who look for that rock-solid sense of trustworthiness from their friends is that other children or adolescents are incapable of being unconditionally loyal.

In the same way that the sailors of old used the North Star to establish their bearings, children need the consistent support of a steady, loving parent. Peers simply cannot be North Stars for one another; the only thing consistent about them is that they wander all over the sky.

Rosie spiraled into a depression as her friends proved themselves unable to provide her with the support and encouragement she needed.

Significance

The fourth stage of attachment is Significance. Just as the true durability of a plant can be measured by the depth of its roots, this stage takes the roots of attachment deeper and promises to help the child feel *held* by her parents even when they aren't physically nearby. When her parents' words and actions make it unquestionably clear that they cherish the unique, one-of-a-kind person their child is, she feels securely connected, knowing how precious she is to them.

When a child *doesn't* have the sense of being special and important to her parents--warts and all--she will pursue

Significance with her friends. (Remember that hit song "I Love You Just the Way You Are" by Billy Joel? We adored that song because it addressed the primal longing to be loved just as we are.)

Rosie had become fixated on her Facebook page because through it she was bombarded with an artificial sense of being special and significant to lots of people. These kinds of sites provide kids with a heady sense of being important because dozens of people—even hundreds or thousands—(most of whom they'll never actually know) want to be their "friends." But it's a smoke-and-mirrors kind of Significance. Ultimately, it's only when the other stages of attachment—Proximity, Sameness, Belonging/Loyalty—are intact that someone truly knows they're special to another. Robert came to realize that Rosie's depression had been fueled by her sense of loneliness, even in the midst of all the cyberspace attention.

Love

The fifth and still deeper stage of attachment is simply Love. Love is the food that nourishes all of us as we make our way in the world. The nourishing affection of a parent fortifies the child as she ventures forth into the world and towards her unfolding personhood. When you can walk through a room where your child is sitting and just smile or tousle her hair while resisting the impulse to ask if she's fed the dog or done her homework, you've given her a dose of Parent Food that feeds her to the core. When a child doesn't feel this elemental, basic love coming from her parent, she will look for it from her peers. And again, peer love is shamelessly inconsistent.

Being Known

The final and deepest stage of attachment is Being Known. If—IF—the attachment has successfully developed up to this point, you will have a child who is open to you, wants you to know his inner world, and tells you his secrets. A child who is deeply connected to his parents wants to confide in them, even if after the fact he finds himself saying, "Oh, man! I promised my buddy I wouldn't tell my folks!" That doesn't mean that a seventeen-year-old will tell you every detail about his latest crush (or that you would want to know!), but it does mean that he will still consider your input and influence worthwhile when he's confused and in need of help with a difficult situation.

When we haven't earned this level of connection—meaning we haven't demonstrated our desire for Proximity, Sameness, Loyalty, Significance, and Love—our children will not tell us what's really going on in their lives. These are lonely and isolated kids who either maintain distance from everyone or, more commonly, share their secrets with—you guessed it—their peers.

After months of confiding in her friends, Rosie came to discover how shallow their connections were and how incapable they were of helping her untangle the stumbling blocks she was encountering in her day-to-day life. Her sense of aloneness led her to look more desperately for pretend connections via her Facebook page. Thankfully, her father sought help in time and began restoring the attachment with his beloved daughter, allowing him to help her turn her life around in a positive direction.

> The people who become truly and deeply close to us let themselves *be known* by us.

All relationships follow this progression of connection

Every relationship will follow along this path of attachment, be it parent-child, friendship, or intimate partnering. We start out a new relationship with a desire to be in the other person's company: **Proximity**. Next we find out that we have things in common such as values and interests: **Sameness**. As the relationship progresses, circumstances inevitably arise in which the other person does something to help us out, showing us that he or she is on our side: **Belonging/Loyalty**. If our connection goes deeper, our friend lets us know that we—and our friendship—are uniquely special to them: **Significance**. Going deeper still, there comes the expression of love, whether it's the love of a solid friendship or the love that develops romantically: **Love**. (As an aside, this is why many love-at-first-sight relationships don't end up lasting forever as we initially believe they will; jumping straight to Love or Being Known without progressing through the previous stages of connection creates a relationship with no backbone or foundation.) And when we look at the people who become truly and deeply close to us, we'll see that they have let themselves be known by us: **Being Known**. Of course, all of this must happen for *both* people in a relationship if there's to be a balanced and healthy connection.

How Robert reconnected with his daughter

So let's get back to Robert. When he came to my office, I listened for a while, and then I outlined these stages of attachment, laying the foundation for the work we would do together. As we spoke, Robert began considering the ways he could rebuild his connection to Rosie. "As far as Proximity goes, one thing I *know* she can't resist is if I offer her a foot rub. She may not want to talk, but she will let me rub her feet while she's watching TV."

"Great," I said. "That's a way for you to invite her to be in your presence, or rather a way to secure an invitation!"

"As for Sameness, I could buy her a Dylan album—we're both huge fans—and leave it on her pillow." I agreed that this would be a way to remind Rosie that she and her dad actually do have things in common.

"I think one thing I really want to let Rosie know is that I'm on her side." He had been especially moved when I was talking about the stage of Belonging/Loyalty, realizing how lonely Rosie must have gotten and how in need she was of feeling that her dad was still her champion.

Robert left with a lot of ideas about the stages of attachment and the ways he might reach out to retrieve Rosie. He was clearly committed to making practical shifts in his interactions with his daughter over the upcoming days.

When we met next, he seemed visibly relieved. The Dylan album was a success, with Rosie apparently quite touched by her dad's surprise. It opened up a twenty-minute conversation (which, Robert realized, was the most they'd actually talked in months) about the lyrics on a couple of the songs, as well as a great discussion about whether it was Dylan's best album. (Dad insisted it was; Rosie disagreed.)

Robert bought a few picture frames with the intention of putting some of Rosie's childhood photos in them. He laid out some photographs and then asked his daughter to help him decide which ones should go with which frame. The simple activity launched a beautiful conversation between them about some things that had happened in her childhood, leading to a bittersweet conversation about Rosie's mom. Robert told me he sensed that this was the beginning of Rosie coming out of her shell.

There were other ways Robert made efforts to reconnect with Rosie over the next few weeks. Things moved along in fits and starts, with moments of closeness alternating with Rosie seeming to push her dad away. During one weekend in particular, he felt as though all the progress they had made was unraveling when she had a falling-out with one of her friends and seemed to take it out on her dad. Robert did his best not to take it personally and to hang in there.

After about three weeks he was rewarded when his daughter finally broke down in tears over something that had happened with another girl. Robert was able to be with Rosie, offering comfort and helping her through as the guiding North Star she so desperately needed. Rosie confessed that she had been feeling depressed a *lot* of the time, and had almost tried cutting (a form of self-injury), which another girl at her school, who was also depressed, said "made the hurt go away." Robert asked Rosie if she'd be willing to come with him for some counseling and for some extra help in getting them back on track, and she finally agreed. With her father's ongoing love and support, Rosie's life turned around, and while their relationship was different from what it had been when she was a little girl doting on her daddy, what they reinvented was real and rock-solid.

Had Robert instead simply focused on Rosie's behavior— forcing her to stay home instead of hanging out with her friends, or making her take down her Facebook page—he might have gotten external compliance, but he wouldn't have gotten his daughter back. He simply would have overpowered her, driving a deeper wedge between them and sending Rosie's depression further underground. The likely outcome would have been cutting, substance abuse, loss of motivation in school, or other maladaptive behaviors.

Children of all ages need to feel securely attached to the captain of the ship in their lives; the deeper the connection, the more the relationship will be able to help children weather the storms of childhood and adolescence.

When my son was younger, he used to think watering the plants—one of his chores— meant getting their leaves wet. I explained to him that roots chase after water and that if a plant is only watered superficially, the roots will stay close to the surface, making it harder for the plant to be healthy and resistant to disease. To be tough enough to withstand droughts and winds, plants need to be watered deeply so the roots will be strong and resilient.

When parents deeply nourish the roots of attachment through all six stages, they give their children the stability they need to grow beautifully and withstand the stressors that are an inevitable part of growing up. In so doing, they truly give children their roots *and* their wings.

A few ideas for promoting healthy attachment
Here are a few ideas for strengthening the parent-child relationship by using the Six Stages of Attachment. For best results, use these strategies one-on-one—one parent with one child. These are just some ideas to get your imagination going!

Proximity
- Surprise your child with an invitation to play UNO or checkers with you.
- Go for a drive without planning your destination, spontaneously making up your route as you go.
- Plan a picnic for the two of you—at a nearby park or in your own backyard!
- Ask your child to teach you something he's good at, whether it's drawing or downloading music; the possibilities are endless.
- Offer to do your daughter's hair in a new way, or give

your son a long back-scratching session.

Sameness

- Rent a movie with an actor the two of you particularly like.
- Take your child to a restaurant that serves something you both drool over.
- Play a game you both really enjoy.
- Invite your child to explain her opinion or point of view about a topic, and let her know the ways you agree.
- Do something you both like, like Ping-Pong, or mini golf.

Belonging/Loyalty

- When your child is overwhelmed with homework, make him a cup of cocoa or rub his shoulders, letting him know you're there to support him.
- Allow your child to hear you explaining to someone else how impressed you are about something he's done—or tell him directly. (This is not the same as praise; it's more about letting him know that you've been inspired by his behavior or positive choices.)
- If your child has a teacher problem, deal with it in a way that doesn't pit you and the teacher against the child. Make it clear that your involvement is about helping to solve the problem and that you're on his side.
- Make sure you come *alongside* your child if he's misbehaved, communicating that you want to see the situation calmly and through his eyes so you can best help him meet his needs in a healthy and acceptable way. (See Chapter 6)
- Thank your child for ways he's helped you out, describing how relieved or grateful you were for his support.

Significance

- Tell her the story of how you chose her name.
- Watch home movies together.
- Look her in the eye, when she least expects it, and tell

her how glad you are she's here.

- Infuse your voice with warmth when you say her name.
- Surprise your child with a card or letter that highlights some of the countless things you appreciate and enjoy about her.

Love

- Tuck a loving note into his lunch box or under his pillow.
- As you walk through the room, tousle his hair and say, "I love you." Then keep walking *without* asking him about something like homework or chores.
- Randomly tell him how his presence lights up your world.
- Tell him how thankful you are to be his parent.
- Slow down and receive any tokens of love he offers, fully taking in those moments together.

Being Known

- When your child speaks—even your three-year-old—make sure you listen, or let them know when you'll be able to if you're busy right now.
- Refrain from offering advice without first letting her say what she needs to say.
- If she reveals a problem, stay open and maintain the sense of being her ally, rather than reacting in ways that might discourage her from opening up to you again.
- Thank her when she's shared her heart with you.
- Fortify connection in the other stages of attachment.

Questions and Suggestions

Question: *My eight-year-old loves to spend time with her daddy—they have a great attachment—but she doesn't seem to be very interested in doing things with me. She doted on me when she was a baby and preschooler, so I think the attachment thing was working then; but now she doesn't seem to want to do anything I suggest. What can I do?*

Suggestion: It's perfectly normal for children to prefer one parent to the other at various stages of their growing up. In addition, every child arrives on earth with her own gifts, interests, talents, and temperaments, so it may be that your husband and daughter's personalities simply overlap a bit more naturally. That's great, but it doesn't mean that you can't have a close connection with her as well. That said, if you're into shopping and she hates it, or if you love movies and she's happiest outdoors, you're going to need to rethink the approaches you're taking to connect with her.

I would urge you to spend a little time doing the following exercise: Take out some paper and write each of the Six Stages of Attachment, leaving a few inches below each stage. Under every stage, brainstorm some ways you can reconnect with your daughter that are enjoyable *from her perspective.* Focus on generating a list of ideas that reflect who *she* is, and what *she* likes, needs, and enjoys. You may not be able to carry a tune, for instance, but she may love music, so beneath the heading of Proximity you may write, "Go see a musical," and under Sameness you might include, "Let her teach me how to play 'Chopsticks' on the piano." By focusing on who your daughter is, you'll discover all kinds of inroads that will help you forge a strong connection with her that reawakens her desire to be close to you.

***

Question: *I like the theory of these Six Stages of Attachment, but my son—who's fourteen but acts like he's twenty-five-- doesn't give much indication that he wants to spend time with me. How can I strengthen the connection if he's not interested?*

Suggestion: First of all, don't be fooled into believing your teen is indifferent or no longer in need of you. Although he may not demonstrate an abundant interest in hanging out with you, it doesn't mean there isn't a deeper longing—and need—to feel connected to you.

I would invite you to spend some time considering who your son is and what he's interested in. Then I would encourage you to think in smaller units of time. While he may not want to go with you to see a movie (a three- or four-hour one-on-one with Mom or Dad may not be appealing to him right now), you can still build attachment with bite-sized moments of being together. Sometimes, my eighteen-year-old son and I play a few rounds of Ping-Pong. Other times we make a cake together. And lots of times I spontaneously offer him some little tidbit about what I admire about him or the ways he's inspired me today. I'm always looking for five- or ten-minute opportunities to feel close, even if it's just the two of us playing with the dog for a few minutes.

These small doses of connection add up; don't underestimate them. They're the glue of the relationship you have with one another. Try sending your son a card in the mail— cute and silly or serious and heartfelt. We all love getting letters, and in this day and age with text messaging and email being the norm, something with a stamp on it addressed especially to him will be memorable. From time to time, cook up something new and delicious. (Food is a great way to build connection and restore dependency with our kids, awakening their primal need to be fed.)

If you've built up a general feeling of goodwill with your son in those ongoing, small experiences, he'll be more willing to spend a few hours with you now and again, especially if you're doing something that's interesting to *him*. Better yet, a short trip somewhere unexpected can do wonders for re-establishing the connection, especially if it's to somewhere new and different— even a new part of the city you don't usually go to—that requires him to lean just a bit more on you in some way.

***

Question: *You say a child moves through these stages over the first six years of life. We adopted our son when he was nearly three years old. Have I lost the chance to build the bonds I would have had if I had been with him from birth?*

Suggestion: Absolutely not. While children move through these stages in their first years of life, as parents we are continually given opportunities to build and rebuild connection through all of these avenues: Proximity, Sameness, Belonging/Loyalty, Significance, Love and Being Known. In fact I have often worked with parents who restored profoundly fractured connection with children now in their twenties or even thirties. These stages and ages are merely suggestions. It's never too late to build attachment from the ground up.

Resist the notion that you missed out on a narrow window of opportunity, and continue strengthening the bond of connection you so clearly have with your son.

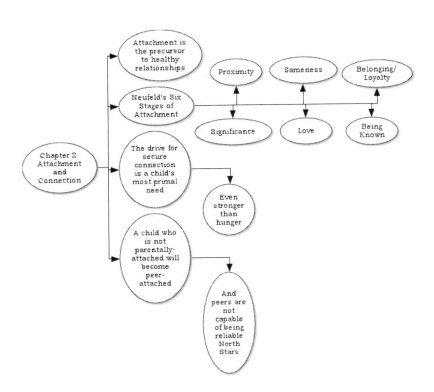

Chapter Three
How to Help Your Kids Have Healthy Relationships with the Members of Their Village

"The main source of children's emotional wellbeing comes from relationships—from their deepest attachments to mothers, fathers, grandparents, and a few cherished others."
Children's Wellbeing Manifesto

Children are meant to be raised in a tribe or village. They're supposed to develop secure attachments to many adults, including aunties, grandfathers, teachers, and elders, all of whom lovingly support and guide them as they move towards becoming young men and women. If all goes well, from the time a baby is born, many adults in his immediate world will be intimately involved in his life. Attachments unfold naturally between a child and the relatives and elders in his village as he grows up in their midst; he naturally develops a closeness that empowers them to contribute to the day-in and day-out job of raising him.

In today's society, a child's grandparents, aunts, uncles, and cousins may live thousands of miles away, often making rare cameo appearances at family gatherings, resulting in their having little influence over the young one as he matures. Without an array of healthy adult connections, the child's attachment needs become focused exclusively on his two parents or, in many cases, the single parent or guardian raising him. Not only does this make bringing up a child more difficult for parents, but it also deprives the youngster of a variety of adults to learn from and confide in as he develops into his own person.

In addition, when divorce impacts a family, a child has to incorporate stepparents, stepsiblings, half-siblings, and all kinds of new extended family members into his life. The divorce rate for second marriages is even higher than for first marriages; having children from a previous marriage can create tremendous stress and strain on a relationship. Children in blended families routinely complain of feeling angry and resentful of the new additions to their family, and tension between stepsiblings and stepparents is commonplace.

The other adults playing a major role in children's lives are their schoolteachers, and unfortunately, many children will at some point have a teacher whom they dislike or fear. With precious few reliably healthy attachments in most children's lives these days, it's debilitating for a youngster to have an unpleasant relationship with a teacher he has to be with for six or seven hours a day; it's even worse if that teacher promotes feelings of shame, loneliness, or inadequacy.

Jacob's very extended family

Jacob was an angry nine-year-old boy when I met him. His parents, Annie and Daniel, had divorced when he was four years old, and Jacob lived primarily with his mother and seven-year-old brother, Teddy, as well as with his stepfather, Mac, who had come into his life two years earlier. Mac had a nine-year-old daughter, Becka, and a twelve-year-old son, Will, who lived with their father and Jacob's mother one week on and one week off. Jacob mostly had weekend contact with his own father, Daniel, who lived thirty minutes away and who had remarried three years earlier, to Marie. Daniel had a two-year-old daughter, Lena, with Marie, who also had a six-year-old son, Marcus, from her first marriage. Jacob had frequent fights with his new stepsiblings as well as with his brother, repeatedly claiming he hated them, hated his new stepparents, and hated his life.

Confused? I sure was. When I initially met with Jacob's parents, I insisted they draw me a family tree indicating the current marriages and clarifying the step- and half-siblings, not to mention the various grandparents (most of whom were fairly present in Jacob's life) and new cousins. My goodness, what this child had been required to integrate in his short life! When his parents reported his chronic anger and lack of cooperation in both households, I wasn't surprised. Still, I knew that Jacob's anger wasn't simply a result of his parents' divorce and their having moved on to new marriages incorporating new children. Many youngsters—including my own son—make it through divorce relatively okay. Kids who feel deeply connected to those who care for them are remarkably resilient. And clearly there are many angry, hurting children being raised by both biological parents in the classic nuclear family arrangement. So while I felt that the crowded cast of characters on the stage of Jacob's life probably contributed to his chronic frustration and anger, I also believed his issues weren't simply a result of their presence in his world.

> Kids who feel deeply connected to those who care for them are remarkably resilient.

I spent my first session with parents Annie and Daniel going over the stages of attachment, as well as explaining their role as captain of the ship in their son's life. In my second session, I decided to try something new to help them—and me— get a better visual on how the relationships in Jacob's life were working. On the left side of a sheet of paper, I listed Neufeld's Six Stages of Attachment: *Proximity, Sameness, Belonging/Loyalty, Significance, Love, and Being Known.* Along the top of the page I listed all the key players in Jacob's life, including his two biological parents, the two stepparents, the siblings, step- and half-siblings, any important aunts, uncles, or grandparents, and his teacher.

I then asked Annie and Daniel to put a number at the intersecting box of each individual and each stage of attachment that would reflect how strong *Jacob* would say that person's connection to him felt *to him* in that area. For instance, if Annie felt Jacob's stepfather, Mac, frequently let Jacob know how special he was to him and that Jacob felt Mac cherished his unique qualities, she might put an eight (on a scale of one to ten) in the box where Mac met Jacob's need for Significance. If she felt his stepfather rarely invited Jacob to spend one-on-one time with him, she would put a two or three in the Proximity/Mac intersecting box. The following table illustrates what their partially completed grid looked like.

How Jacob would rate these relationships	Mom	Dad	Mac	Marie	Teacher	Teddy	Becka & Will	Grandpa Steve	Grandma Bess
Proximity	7	6	3	2	4	8	5	7	9
Sameness	5	5	2	5	5	7	6	7	7
Belonging/ Loyalty	3	3	2	1	3	5	4	8	9
Significance	6	5	4	4	5	5	4	9	9
Love	7	6	4	3	4	7	4	9	9
Being Known	7	6	3	3	3	6	4	8	9

While assigning numerical values to relationships was, in and of itself, a bit far-fetched, I used this exercise to give Annie and Daniel a visual sense of where Jacob felt he was being seen, enjoyed, and cherished—and where he wasn't. When a child spends a significant amount of time in the company of those whom he feels don't understand him or enjoy his presence, it wears down his spirit and diminishes his joy. While no one would reasonably expect a person to instantly bond with a child just because they fell in love with the child's parent, when someone chooses to become a stepparent, they are (hopefully) also choosing to forge the most genuine connection possible with their new partner's child. Not only is this in the child's best interests, it also unites the family in a way that helps the marriage survive the unavoidable adjustments that will have to be made.

Looking at the grid they'd created, Annie and Daniel became immediately aware of how fragile most of Jacob's connections were, including the one with his teacher. They were especially struck by the absence of any sense of connection through Loyalty their son probably felt with each of them, not to mention with the other significant adults in his life. Jacob's parents realized that he had not only been inundated with trying to weave new people into his world in a very short time, he was also somewhat like a passenger on a ship without a secure captain at the helm most of the time. Clearly, this was one of the underlying reasons their young son felt angry so often. He was functioning outside of close connection and attachment *and* had competing attachments—new siblings and new mates—vying for his parents' attention on a constant basis.

> When a child spends a significant amount of time in the company of those whom he feels don't understand him or enjoy his presence, it wears down his spirit and diminishes his joy.

I worked with Annie and Daniel to implement new approaches for dealing with Jacob when he was upset, which I'll introduce in subsequent chapters. But before teaching them how to deal with their son's frustration and anger, I needed to help them establish a solid sense of connection with Jacob, so he would actually be receptive to their efforts to help him when he was frustrated and angry. Unless his parents could awaken his natural instincts to look to them for help and guidance, their efforts to draw him out of his anger and elicit his cooperation would continue to be problematic.

The initial focal point of my work with Jacob's family was to help his parents strengthen their connection to him. We looked especially at the areas they had indicated were the weakest. I then discussed how Annie and Daniel might help their spouses fortify *their own* attachments to Jacob. I felt strongly that if each of the stepparents put even small amounts of time into creating authentic relationships with Jacob, it would significantly improve life within each family.

I met with the stepparents as well, giving them space to express their ambivalence and frustrations as they attempted to forge loving families with their new spouses, which they had hoped would include a cooperative and well-adjusted Jacob. Rather than criticizing them or fueling their feelings of guilt and failure, I came *alongside* Marie and Mac, who had been struggling to dance around Jacob's anger while building new marriages and families with his father and mother. By giving them practical steps to take towards building attachment with Jacob, they felt empowered to create a solid connection with this young boy.

When I checked in with these families two months later, I discovered that both families had gotten on a much better track. There had been many setbacks, and they still weren't describing themselves as the Brady Bunch, but they were moving in a good direction. As the stepparents worked to create authentic relationships with Jacob, starting with Proximity but not rushing the attachment process, they were better able to help Jacob and his siblings forge durable connections with one another. As Jacob and his brothers and sisters each felt their need for connection being met by their parents and stepparents, the natural byproduct was that the relationships between the children improved, as well.

Helping Jacob and his teacher connect

I asked Annie and Daniel to share what they had learned in our work together with Jacob's teacher, Ms. Davis, so she could try to build a more functional relationship with him. She, too, had been frustrated with his unhappiness at school and was thrilled to get some ideas for making things better. In addition, I encouraged Jacob's parents to "match make" between Ms. Davis and their son. I suggested that they try to regularly email Ms. Davis about things she did during school that Jacob said he liked, whether it was the way she read a story after lunch, the funny things she said about the class gerbil, or the way she laughed. Similarly, I asked Daniel and Annie to make sure they shared with Jacob any positive things his teacher said about him. "Jacob, Ms. Davis *loves* the way you tell a joke; she told us she often tries to repeat them to the other teachers, but they're never as funny as when you tell them." Or, "Your teacher called to say you had the cleverest ideas today in science, when you were talking about the different ways to melt an ice cube."

When his parents began pointedly feeding both Ms. Davis and Jacob with positive impressions of the other, the relationship between them grew more natural and friendly, and Jacob's complaints about her "stupid homework assignments" and "lame rules" seemed to diminish significantly.

Jacob's complicated family issues were by no means a simple fix, and there still remain many unresolved issues and frustrating moments. But by focusing on building stronger attachments with the key players in his life—rather than attempting to improve his attitude or simply give him the chance to vent his anger—his parents greatly improved the day-to-day life of more than a dozen people impacted by their unhappy son. Even more, they offered Jacob the enrichment and security that comes when a child has a number of secure and loving attachments.

Children need as many healthy adult connections as possible. This not only requires us to consider which of our friends, relatives, teachers, and neighbors might be possible candidates to play more important roles in our son or daughter's life; it also means we ourselves need to sign up to be that adult for children other than our own.

When my dear friend Jenny passed away, her children were six and eight years old. They are still an important part of my life. Although they live in Europe, they visit us every year or two, and we stay in touch through telephone, email, and online chats. My friend Sandy's children were six, eight, and ten when their young mother passed away. When I'm lucky, they're dropped off at my house once a week to play and do homework with a little help from my son. These children will always be in my life, if I have any say, and there are many other children and teens in my world—kids whose parents are alive and well—for whom I'm an important auntie.

I know that by putting energy into the lives of other children I'm creating a bond that benefits us all. Naturally, some of us are more into kids than others, but I do believe that many of us have forgotten the responsibility we share for helping raise the children in our extended families, neighborhoods, and communities. So many modern societal problems point glaringly to the lack of connection experienced by kids these days. The rampant escalation of desperate measures that kids take—school shootings being the tragic pinnacle—underscore the truth that it really *does* take a village to raise a child.

Even though most of our living situations bear no resemblance to an actual village, children still do best when we grow up with a variety of strong and loving attachments to caring adults around us. As parents, we need to foster connections with people who have the potential to be important to our kids as they grow up and move towards their own personhood. And as members of the tribe of our extended family, neighborhood, or community, it's essential that we also sign up to *be* an important adult to other children. When we help *all* the kids in our lives to have healthy relationships with as many sane and caring grownups as possible, we help send them on towards a life where they're joyful, resilient, and authentically themselves.

Questions and Suggestions

Question: *My daughter absolutely refuses to stay with a babysitter. I don't have any close family members to watch her, and I need a break. How can I get her to stay happily with a sitter?*

Suggestion: Focus on matchmaking a relationship between your daughter and one or two reliable babysitters. Invite them to dinner (you'll probably need to pay for their time, but it will be worth it). Refer frequently to the babysitters by name in conversation so your daughter starts to feel that they're part of her extended family. Go with your daughter and a sitter to the park or out for ice cream prior to leaving the two of them on their own. Try to arrange it so the first few times your daughter is alone with the sitter it's only for a short period. Provide the sitter with one or two games or activities that your daughter hasn't seen so it might be easier to distract her, but if she needs to cry, make sure the babysitter you've chosen can lovingly allow her to do so.

There are some who feel your daughter might be manipulating you (and therefore, in charge) by her refusal to stay with the babysitter. Only you know whether or not that's true. Undoubtedly, your daughter prefers your company, but it's ultimately in her best interest—not to mention yours—that she knows she's safe and can have fun with other adults, as well as you. So take charge, acknowledge that she prefers you *and* that you'll be back soon, and leave her in the care of someone she's had the chance to get to know a bit more naturally, and you should be able to enjoy your well-deserved break!

***

Question: *I have an eight-year-old stepson who spends every other weekend with my husband and me. I know he misses his mom a lot when he's with us, and I do my best to help him feel comfortable; but as much as I've tried to win him over, he just doesn't seem interested in having a relationship with me. My husband says it's just a matter of time, but I feel like there ought to be some way I can help move this process along.*

Suggestion: I'm glad to hear you want to do what you can to build a relationship with your stepson, and while I agree with your husband that ultimately it is out of your hands as to how receptive the boy will be, I believe there are most certainly things you can do to invite him to share a connection with you.

It's going to be important that you create your own unique relationship with him, one that doesn't feel intrusive or cause him to feel disloyal to his mother. Look through the stages of attachment and consider how you could build something with a real foundation, beginning with letting him know you like to be around him (Proximity).

Ask your husband to help you generate a list of twenty things your stepson enjoys. Think about activities you could create from this list, especially if they're interests you two have in common (Sameness).

If you both like chocolate, you could visit a chocolatier for sample tastings. If he's into action figures, ask him the names of his guys and what powers they have. Don't be pushy or overly in his face. Just gently approach him in a comfortable way. The most important thing to keep in mind is that you're offering these activities to him without an agenda or expectation that he'll be responsive. If *you* can be okay with him taking his time to warm up to you, you'll give him the space to build a bridge to you in his own way.

***

Question: *Our children, ages three, seven, and eleven, rarely see their grandparents—my wife's mother and father. They live on the other side of the country and usually visit us once a year. When Grandma Lea and Grandpa Jim come to visit, they're very excited to see their grandkids, but because they don't know them very well, our children aren't very affectionate or open with them. I know this disappoints Lea and Jim. Do you have any suggestions on how to fast-track their connection so Grandma and Grandpa don't feel like strangers to our children?*

Suggestion: I would encourage the grandparents to stay in touch with letters, phone calls, and even email, if appropriate. But in this situation, there are also things that you, as your children's parents, can do to help bridge the gap.

Initiate family phone calls every two weeks—or video conferencing, if you're computer savvy! Give Grandma and Grandpa a list of each child's special interests or latest activities and help them come up with ways to incorporate those into their communications. Mention Grandma and Grandpa frequently, and make sure you have photos of them *with your children* prominently displayed. Call Lea and Jim if one of your children has a special moment so your kids experience you weaving them into your day-to-day lives.

When the grandparents come to visit, it's fine if they bring little gifts for each child, but I would encourage them to focus less on buying special things (which is always tempting to do) and more on playing games, taking walks, and reading stories with each child, (one-on-one as much as possible,) to forge real connections.

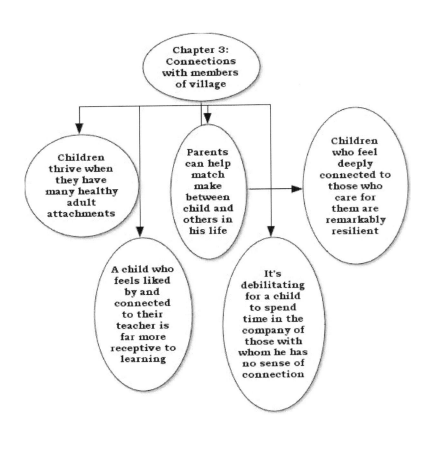

Chapter 3: Connections with members of village

Children thrive when they have many healthy adult attachments

Parents can help match make between child and others in his life

Children who feel deeply connected to those who care for them are remarkably resilient

A child who feels liked by and connected to their teacher is far more receptive to learning

It's debilitating for a child to spend time in the company of those with whom he has no sense of connection

Chapter Four
Creating an Unshakable Connection With Your Kids

Allowing children to feel truly seen and heard, without being judged, is one of the greatest gifts we can give them.

Early in my career I often worked with children who had been in counseling with prominent therapists but had, surprisingly, made little progress. Many times, within a week or two of our working together, their parents were reporting dramatic improvement in problematic behaviors that had been unresponsive to approaches made by my seasoned colleagues. I was relatively new to the field and couldn't explain why I was having so much success when far more experienced therapists seemed unable to make any headway with certain children. I finally realized that the operative feature of my approach wasn't my impressive years of experience but the fact that the children I worked with got the clear message that I was genuinely curious about finding out who they really were. I was leaning forward in the process of getting to know them; and this involved heartfelt, open-minded listening, and an unmistakable desire to be fully present with them.

> The children got the clear message that I was genuinely curious to find out who they really were.

Damian

Fifteen-year-old Damian lived with his father, Brian; his mother, Jane; and his eight-year-old sister, Trina. Damian's parents told me that he had become unreachable, having rejected their repeated and earnest efforts to connect with him over the last few years. "We had resigned ourselves to the fact that Damian far preferred his friends to us; we just accepted that we were no longer very interesting to him and that his pulling away was normal teen behavior. Even when he was home, he mostly stayed in his own world with his iPod headphones practically glued to his ears."

They explained that this was not inherently a problem, except that recently Damian seemed to be more irritable, his grades were slipping, and he seemed especially unkind to his little sister. Jane expressed her concern about the effect that Damian's sullen mood and perpetual anger were having on her daughter.

Jane and Brian attended my workshop on parenting adolescents and learned ways to strengthen their connection to Damian and to address the chronic frustration that had fueled his anger. Things improved in their household significantly, but Brian called me a few weeks later asking for some private sessions. "We're definitely doing a lot better, but Damian still doesn't seem all that willing to open up with his mom or me. I think he needs us more than he acknowledges. I feel like he's a bit lost, swimming upstream with all those other confused ninth graders, and that he could really use a North Star. But he's a tough nut to crack; he opens up a little bit and then clams up. Jane and I feel that he needs someone to talk to, since he won't tell us a thing."

I was impressed by this father's desire to make things great instead of just better, and so I invited Brian and Jane in for a session to talk things over.

"Things really are a lot better," Jane said. "But I think Damian's kind of trapped behind his adolescent bravado. It feels like he's waiting for us to draw him out. I used to believe that when kids became teens we needed to let them drift off with their friends, but I understand—after your workshop—how much he still needs his parents, in a different way. We're just not sure how to be there for him in the way he needs us."

I suggested that the remedy Jane and Brian were looking for would be found by examining how strong their attachment with Damian was, particularly in the last phase—Being Known. We brainstormed creative ways that each of them could deepen their relationship with Damian by spending physical time together (Proximity) and by emphasizing activities and interests they shared with him (Sameness). We talked about ways they could advocate for Damian and make it clear that they were on his side and rooting for his success (Belonging/Loyalty), whether this was in academics, sports, or just day-to-day life. I asked them to look for more ways they could individually let Damian know how much they loved and appreciated him just as he is (Significance and Love).

When it came to Being Known, I spent a fair bit of time role-playing conversations with Jane and Brian, since I had the feeling they were tripping over themselves in their interactions with their son. "Show me how a typical conversation with Damian might go," I said to them. "I'll be Damian, and we'll start with you, Jane. Pick an opening that you think might lead to a more in-depth conversation with your son."

Jane, as Mom: "So, Damian, what'd you do in school today? Do you have any homework?"

I said to Jane, "Hang on, Jane! Do you believe this kind of opening is going to inspire your son to engage in a deep conversation? Stay away from opening with an agenda, like homework! Let's try again!"

Jane (laughing at herself) replied, "Whoops! Okay, Susan, I think I've got it. Let's try it again."

Jane, as Mom: "Damian, tell me—what is it about the Lakers that makes you love them so much?"

Susan, as Damian: "Where do I start? They've got Kobe, and they just signed on this new guy, Pau Gasol. He's awesome. But it's not just that . . ." I continued on for a while with great animation.

Jane, as Mom: "That's great, honey. Cool."

Jane stepped out of character for a moment and said, "I have to admit, my eyes start glazing over pretty quickly when he starts talking about basketball. I don't know what else to even ask about it!"

I reassured her, "You don't need to start studying up on the Lakers, Jane. The point isn't to be someone you're not or to pretend you have an interest in something that isn't genuine. But where you *can* go with this is in being fully present with your son for a few minutes, regardless of what he's talking about. Join him in his excitement and passion about something that wakes him up. It's not about the Lakers—it's about connecting."

Jane laughed a little and said, "Okay, that's good! Let me try saying this":

Jane, as Mom: "Is this year's team better than it was last year?"

Susan, as Damian: "In a lot of ways it is. I mean, it's not like the Lakers when
Shaq was on the team, but they've got a lot of new talent and some really strong players."

Jane, as Mom: "I love listening to you talk about the Lakers, Damian. You know so much about them."

Susan, as Damian: "You got that right!"

I suggested to Jane that we stop the role-play for a few minutes so we could talk a little bit about it. "What was that like for you, Jane?"

"At first it was hard. I'm glad you stopped me on my first try; more often than not, that's exactly the kind of conversation starter I use—asking about homework or school—and I usually get one-word answers. It felt unnatural to keep asking things about the Lakers, since I don't really know anything about them. But with you coaching me, I managed to fumble along, and I could see how Damian would be more responsive if I had this kind of conversation with him more often."

Brian chimed in, "It was neat watching you, Jane, because even though I could see that you were struggling to ask good questions, it was so clear that *what* you asked wasn't all that important. I definitely think Damian would love to have this kind of conversation with you. He's so used to us talking to him about tasks or giving him unwanted advice that I think he would open up a whole lot more if we had these kinds of conversations with him more often."

Encouraged by Brian's responsiveness to the role-play, I said, "Let's do one with you, Brian. I'll be Damian, and you be you."

Susan, as Damian: "So, Dad, I need you to sign this test. I got a D. It's no big deal, but you've gotta sign it."

Brian, as Dad: "Sure, Damian. I'll be happy to sign it. But, what happened, son? You don't usually get D's in math, do you?"

Susan, as Damian: "Like I said, it's no big deal, Dad. Why don't you trust me? Can't you just sign it without making it a federal case?"

Brian, as Dad: "I'm not making it a federal case, Damian. But I *am* your dad. And I want to know what's going on so I can help you."

Susan, as Damian: "Whatever. Just forget it."

Brian asked me to stop the role-play. "This is going where I don't want it to go, and it's exactly what happens a lot of the time when Damian talks to me. I want him to feel that I'm listening and not shutting him down; but in real life, I seem to say all the things that make him clam up. Help!"

"Okay," I said. "Let's switch roles, and I'll try to take it in a different direction."

Brian, as Damian: "Dad, you've gotta sign this test. I got a D."

Susan, as Dad: "Okay, son. What is it, the teacher makes you get these things signed if you get a D or something?"

Brian, as Damian: "Yeah, it's super lame. It used to be if you got an F you had to get it signed, but now he's making you do it for D's. It's so stupid."

Susan, as Dad: "I get the feeling you aren't too excited about having to get us to sign it."

Brian, as Damian: "You got that right."

Susan, as Dad: "It must be hard, not knowing if this is one of those times you're going to get one of our well-meaning parent lectures."

Brian, as Damian: "Yup."

Susan, as Dad: "I get it, son. And you know, it *is* a tough call, 'cause one part of me does want to see if I can help you somehow. But I know when I do that, it can come off like I'm upset or giving you advice you don't really want to hear."

Brian, as Damian: "Yeah. I hate it when you guys go off on me. It's no big deal—it's just one D!"

Susan, as Dad: "Well, I appreciate you wanting to reassure me about the test, Damian. It sounds like this wasn't an important test, then?"

Brian, as Damian: "Not really. I mean, I actually thought I was gonna get a B. I thought I knew everything on the test. He's such a hard grader. The teacher's a total jerk."

Susan, as Dad: "That's a drag. It's got to be tough when you know you tried hard to do well."

Brian, as Damian: "I did. It sucks that he's so mean."

Susan, as Dad: "I'm sorry, son. It's not easy having class every day with a teacher you don't really like, or trying to do well on a test and then finding out you got a D."

I suggested to Brian that we pause the role-play. "So, is this going the way it usually goes, Brian?"

"No way. I wouldn't usually get this much information out of him. It's amazing. When I hear the way you're being the dad—not judging or giving unwanted advice—I find myself naturally wanting to tell you more. Where would you go from here?"

I told Brian that I'd follow this same style, rephrasing and putting into words what Damian seemed to be feeling instead of focusing on why he got the D or making "helpful" suggestions that would inevitably turn him off and end the conversation. (For more on this, see Chapter 6.) "I'd be looking to help Damian get the sense that I'm on his side—that I'm coming *alongside* him, wanting to understand what this experience has been like for him—rather than coming *at* him, which turns this conversation into a power struggle. I want to show Damian that I can manage my own reactions or disappointment and stay present through what could be an unpleasant conversation."

I role-played some other scenarios with Jane and Brian, and then I had them practice with one another. When I heard from them a few weeks later, they said they felt much more connected to their son; they reported that he was telling them more personal things, and already he seemed to walk around in a much better mood.

Kids want to be able to tell us the truth

Kids want and need parents who are able to receive what they have to say, whether it's good news or bad; but first they test us to determine whether we're going to be able to handle what they want to tell us. We often unconsciously send our kids the message that we can't or don't want to hear them by interrupting, advising, criticizing, and questioning them instead of listening attentively (and with our lips together!).

A child who has discovered that her parents can hear her truth is far less burdened. She feels an authentic closeness with them that nourishes and supports her through the ups and downs of life. Keeping a secret from people we love creates a sense of disconnection from them. In the context of a strong attachment, this distance becomes intolerable. Still, we need to send our kids the clear message that we can handle their truth—and that we *want* to.

Neck up versus neck down

I often explain to parents that a child's communication has two parts: the part delivered from the neck up, and the part that comes from the neck down. When a child, speaking from the neck up, says, "I hate my little brother," we're often tempted to *reply* from the neck up: "How can you say that? He adores you!" This type of interaction stems from logic and focuses exclusively on the content, leaving out the more important—but perhaps encoded—emotions underneath the words.

When our children's words trouble us, it's easy to end up ignoring the real message—the *feelings* that they're attempting to express in language. When this happens, we often end up arguing with them, using logic in an attempt to set their thinking right. They feel misunderstood, and the conversation comes to a screeching halt. We need to avoid being tricked into believing that our youngsters' *words* contain their actual *message*. Our job is to be the translator for our kids, to help them express what they're *feeling* (neck down) with words that reflect the truth of what they're *experiencing*.

> When our children's words trouble us, it's easy to end up ignoring the real message—the *feelings* that they're attempting to express in language.

Still more ways to build connection

Our children desperately want to know that we genuinely want to understand them better. Parents often complain that they're overworked, spread too thin and that they simply don't have the luxury of spending hours of one-on-one time with their sons or daughters. But strengthening the parent-child attachment is not a matter of time. Whether you have one child or five, you can still find ten minutes a week to hide out with each of them in your room—or theirs—putting a "Do Not Disturb" sign on the door, telling jokes, making up a song or just snuggling. Sure, your children will naturally want more of that and won't want to see their special time with you come to an end, but that's a good thing. You can let them know that you also want more time with each of them, and you can begin generating ideas with them for fun things you can do together.

When your child asks for your attention and you can give it, try to offer it completely. Be generous. A child feels the difference between attention you give willingly and attention you give because it's been demanded of you. While she's talking, notice the color of her eyes. Rephrase what she's saying so she knows you're actually processing what she's telling you. Allow her to see that you're digesting what she's told you as you pause now and again to mull over something she's said.

If you don't have time for your child right then, tell her when you will. If the best you have is just a few minutes to spare, let her know that you're hers for that time. You might say, "I wish I had longer," but at least for those three minutes be all ears and fully present rather than saying, "I'm listening! I hear you!" while simultaneously checking your email. And again, if you truly can't give her your attention right now, explain that you'd like to, and offer a time when you *can* be available—ideally, sometime in the next few hours.

Another way of creating an unshakable connection with your children or teens is to ask them their opinion about something, and then encourage them to elaborate. Stop and reflect on what they have said, demonstrating your sincere desire to understand life from their vantage point. Show them you really want to know what they think about a piece of music or an actor, or why they think chocolate ice cream is better than vanilla. Be hungry to discover more of who they are, and let them know what a delight it is to get to know them as they blossom into their true selves.

Ask your kids questions like "What was the most challenging thing you did this week?" "What grown up do you know that you think would make a fantastic teacher?" or "Finish this sentence: Today I daydreamed about _____." Rather than asking a typical parent question such as "How was school?" and getting the usual response of "Fine," try asking open-ended questions where you are listening with eager anticipation for their response. Such open questions promote tremendous connection between people.

By setting the intention to get to know our kids, and then following through by capturing random moments when we can discover more about who they are and who they're becoming, we set the stage for unshakable connections with them that will carry us through the ups and downs of daily life.

Questions and Suggestions

Question: *On paper, the idea of letting our kids tell us things without judging sounds great. But in real life, it's hard to imagine having conversations with my kids on touchy subjects without jumping in and offering advice to them. How can I do this?*

Suggestion: Your question speaks to the reality that all parents face: Before we actually have children, none of us understands what we're in for. It's easy to wax philosophical about some other person's parenting predicament and how effectively we'd handle it—until it lands on our own doorstep.

I'll be honest here; there are many conversations I've had to have with my son where it has not been easy for me to remain cool, calm, and collected. The reality is that it often *isn't* easy to hear our kids tell us things that trigger our worry, fear, or anger. Try practicing with the little things—your daughter belatedly admitting she took the last cookie or your son confessing that he doesn't *really* like Aunt Martha's birthday present. With practice, you'll become more comfortable handling these difficult conversations. And keep remembering the payoff to letting your kids truly offload what's on their mind with you: It's far better to be *in* the loop than *out* of it; and when you really know what your kids are going through, you'll be in the best position possible to offer them the help they need from you. (Read about Act I and Act II in Chapter 6 for more on handling those difficult conversations.)

***

Question: *My eight-year old daughter says things all the time that she knows aren't true—things like, "I know you love Louie (her little brother) more than me." Can you explain how I would use the Neck Up/ Neck Down idea with a child who says things that are obviously untrue?*

Suggestion: The key to using the Neck up/ Neck down image is to picture a child's *words* as coming from the Neck up, and the *feelings* that pushed the words out as coming from the Neck down. Another way of thinking about this is to imagine that the content of what she's saying is a function of the verbal, left side of her brain, while the emotions come more from the feeling, right side of her brain. While it can be tempting to focus on the words a child uses, when we do, we often miss the real message hiding *behind* the words. It's as if you're knocking on the left side of her brain—attempting to engage her with logic and language—when nobody's home because she's over in her right brain at the moment.

Rather than getting hung up on *what* your daughter says, concentrate on discovering what's going on beneath the surface. Instead of trying to convince her that her Neck up statements are inaccurate, focus on helping her get in touch with the real meaning behind her words—the Neck down part of her message. The more you do this, the less she'll be inclined to make those dramatic statements. As you'll see in upcoming chapters, when you avoid getting entangled in debates about *what* a child is saying, you'll be better able to address the underlying issue.

***

Question: *My daughter lives with her mother in another city, and I only see her on holidays and summer vacations. Is it possible to build an unshakable connection with a child I don't see every day?*

Suggestion: Of course it's possible, but it will take special effort on your part to forge that bond. Your situation is challenging, and unfortunately it is becoming more commonplace.

This is what I recommend to parents who don't have regular physical contact with their children: Set an intention within yourself *and* with your daughter that you are her dad and that she is your priority, whether she's with you or far away. Let her know how much it matters to you that the two of you find a way to stay connected and close, and then start taking action to reflect your commitment.

Here's where technology comes in handy. I would make sure your daughter has a cell phone, a web cam for her computer (or access to one, even at Kinko's), and an email address. I won't elaborate on how to use these—I'm fairly certain you know—but there are many experts who can teach you if you need technical advice. Skype is fantastic for staying in touch, but there are all kinds of ways including regular text messaging, emailing photos, and twitter. You can even record short video clips of yourself telling her a joke, or elaborating on something from one of your recent conversations. You may even want to consider one of the new Smartphones that let you do video chat.

I would set up a schedule of some kind that reflects your desire to contact her every day or two. It is *your* responsibility to contact *her*; do not make it her job to reach out to you. You're the parent; she's the child. Recognize that she has her own life and activities and that she may not be reachable. Do not get upset or angry with her if she doesn't answer her phone or respond to your emails, and don't push it or lay a guilt trip on her if she's busy or brief with you. What's important is that *you* continue reaching towards her whether she responds in the way you think she should or not.

Send her things in the mail. Kids love getting cards, letters, and little packages; and this will be a very practical gesture to let her know you're thinking of her and making the extra effort it obviously takes—beyond leaving a phone message—that tells her she's on your mind.

Try creating some kind of ritual that reflects what she's into these days. If you know she likes Hannah Montana, send her a little Hannah Montana trivia question. (Yes, this kind of thing exists on the Internet.) If she's into riddles, see if she wants to set up a riddle club where the two of you send each other riddles and try to solve them together.

The operant bit here is to make sure the way you connect is enticing and fun and that staying connected to Dad doesn't end up feeling to her like a chore or a burden. By clearly demonstrating your desire to stay close to your daughter, you'll be able to forge a rock-solid connection, regardless of the physical distance between the two of you.

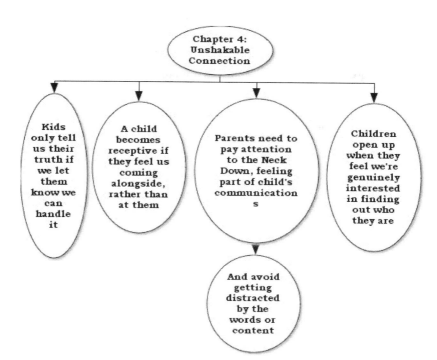

Chapter Five
Helping Kids Deal With Frustration

*"Every life and every childhood is filled with frustrations;
we cannot imagine it otherwise, for even the best mother
cannot satisfy all her child's wishes and needs. It is not the
suffering caused by frustration, however, that leads to
emotional illness, but rather the fact that the child is
forbidden by the parents to experience and articulate this
suffering—the pain felt at being wounded."*
Alice Miller

Childhood is full of frustrating moments. Nature has designed life for children in such a way as to guarantee that they'll have their wishes denied many times a day. Children are small, physically disadvantaged, in need of support that isn't always available, and desirous of all sorts of things that their caretakers determine aren't good for them. As loving parents, we hate it when our kids cry, and we'll jump through hoops to keep their tears at bay. We buy them the toys they can't live without, force their big sisters to play Barbies with them, or let them stay up late even though we know they'll be tired the next day. We justify our manipulations of people, events, and rules on our children's behalf with the false belief that when we eliminate their frustrations, we're demonstrating our love. But the truth is, when we prevent children from experiencing frustration, we're crippling them from developing the vital life skill of learning to adapt, which is an ability they'll need throughout their adult lives.

Rather than coldly admonishing a child to "deal with it" when she's upset, parents need to help the frustrated child along to what psychologist Gordon Neufeld[1] calls the Wall of Futility. The child needs to feel her real feelings of sadness and find her tears. And *when* the child—often with your help—is able to come to her tears about whatever she wants and can't have or whatever is broken and can't be fixed, she becomes able to move on—*to adapt.*

When we prime a child's tears, softening our voice and

acknowledging how hurt she's feeling because big sister said "I don't want to play with you," we help this little girl's disappointment find expression and release. Once the tears come, the child is soon off and running, looking for something or someone else to play with, but this time with one more successful adaptation under her belt. She has discovered that while life may not always unfold to her liking, she can *adapt* to it and find her way back to joy.

Why Frustration fuels aggression

When parents intervene because their child is frustrated—believing they're doing so out of love and care—they prevent him from learning the lesson of adaptation. As a result, when their child experiences something upsetting later in his life, either he demands that circumstances bend to his will or he becomes aggressive. Like so many people, he grows up to become an adult who cannot cope when things don't conform to his liking—like people who demand service or recompense when they're disappointed or who numb themselves with substances or distractions just so they can cope with life's difficult moments.

> When parents intervene because their children are frustrated—believing they're doing so out of love and care—they prevent them from learning the lesson of adaptation.

Think about it. Have you ever been in a relationship that clearly wasn't going to work out, and instead of letting it go, you found yourself obsessing over and over about what happened, talking about it with friends, sending one last email, or writing furiously about it in your journal?

Sex and the City and the Wall of Futility

One of the biggest hits in recent times was the book *He's Just Not That into You,* which stemmed from a hugely popular episode of *Sex and the City* in which a male character decodes the behavior of one of the women's recent dates. After hearing the other three women analyze and explain why Miranda's recent date hasn't yet called to ask her out again, the male expert is asked for his take on the guy's disappearance. When he tells them the truth from his perspective as a man, "Want to know what I think? He's just not that into you," the three girlfriends desperately try to dismiss his opinion. "Don't be ridiculous! He probably had to go out of town . . . is obviously wrapped up in work . . . surely he has that flu that's been going around." But Miranda gets a huge smile on her face. She realizes he's telling the truth and thanks him enthusiastically. Having made her peace with the harsh reality, she can now adapt and move on.

Sometimes we aren't as quick-witted as Miranda; and instead of "getting it" immediately and moving on, we continue the conversation with whatever friend will endure it. In the end, it's only when we find our tears, *when we hit the Wall of Futility* and begin to grieve our loss, that we can accept and move on. Whether it's a relationship, a promotion, or a million other circumstances that don't unfold as we had hoped, *our ability to live joyful and successful lives depends on our ability to adapt.* One of the greatest gifts we can give our children is to help them find feel their sadness fully when they're frustrated. Tears actually release stress hormones and toxins; as usual, Mother Nature knows what she's doing.

What happens when children *don't* feel their sadness or find their tears, and we parents don't bend the world to their liking? Unresolved frustration produces aggression. Whether it's verbal or physical, a child who is prevented from getting what he wants and who lacks the ability to adapt will become aggressive. And when we "up the ante" and punish the child by taking more and more things away, we simply move him towards either increasing his aggressive behavior or hardening his heart.

DABDA: The Stages of Grief

Another way of thinking about this process is to consider *DABDA*, the acronym for the five stages of grief: Denial, Anger, Bargaining, Depression, and Acceptance. While DABDA refers to the journey a person goes through when faced with the death of a loved one, it is equally applicable to what needs to happen for humans to successfully deal with any loss or disappointment.

When things don't go the way the child wants—Santa doesn't bring the new bike, big brother won't let her tag along, Grandma can't come to her birthday—she needs to find her way to Acceptance. A frustrated child is stuck in Anger and Bargaining, and she needs the help of a loving caregiver to walk her through her feelings so she can come to Acceptance and move on.

Most of us—including children-- begin with Denial when we first encounter the possibility that what we want isn't going to happen. We then need to help the child through his Anger, rather than getting stuck in the negotiating (Bargaining) he'll use to try to make things happen the way he wants. What the child really needs from us is to help him experience his sadness (Depression), as he comes to more deeply feel the ramifications of his wish not coming true. As we language a child's disappointment and sorrow around the loss of his desire, and endure the experience of him hitting that Wall of Futility, we help him move towards Acceptance—and Adaptation.

As painful as it is to experience loss, whether it's a loved one's death or moving to a new home, what can be even harder to endure is limbo: not knowing *if* Grandma's going to recover or not, or whether Mom's new job is going to come through and make us move to a new town. Similarly, when we try to avoid frustrating our child by hemming and hawing about whether they will or won't get something, we increase their suffering. It's better to walk them to their sadness and tears, and help them learn to adapt.

Four ways parents approach a frustrated child
Let's look at a dialogue between a mom and her ten-year-old daughter. What follows are four versions: one in which Mom does nothing and the already resilient child naturally adapts; one in which Mom bends the universe to line up with what her daughter wants (and *doesn't* give her the chance to practice adaptation); one in which Mom does nothing; and one in which Mom moves her daughter towards adapting by helping her find her tears.

Scenario: *Daisy comes to Mom and asks to watch a TV show. Mom has decided that because it's late and near bedtime, it's not a good idea.*

VERSION 1: Mom does nothing, and Daisy adapts on her own.

Daisy: "So, can I watch that show, Mom? Please? PLEASE?!"

Mom: "I'm afraid not, sweetie."

Daisy: "Darn it. Oh well, I'm gonna go figure out what I'm wearing tomorrow. Audrey and I promised each other we'd dress totally in green from head to toe!"

Mom: "Wow. Sounds like big fun!"

Daisy has adapted. Most likely, she has had enough prior experience with handling frustration that she's able to quickly deal with her disappointment and move on.

VERSION 2: Mom, attempting to spare her daughter from experiencing frustration, prevents her from hitting the "Wall of Futility."

Daisy: "So, can I watch that show, Mom? Please? PLEASE?!"

Mom: "Honey, I don't think it's a good idea." *[Child senses Mom's indecisiveness.]*

Daisy: "C'mon Mom. Why can't I watch it?"

Mom: "Because it's late, Daisy, and you have to get up in the morning for school."

Daisy: "I'll get up! It's not a problem, Mom. I'll go right to sleep after I watch it and get up just fine."

Mom: "Actually, sweetheart, on Monday I did let you watch something later than usual and you ended up all wound up and not able to go to sleep for a long time. Don't you remember? You were really tired and hard to wake up the next morning."

Daisy: "But Mom, that was different. I was wound up when the show started 'cause I'd had a bad day. And that show was more exciting than this one."

Mom: "Well, darling, I just don't think it's a good idea.

[Again, note the uncertainty.]

Daisy: "You are SO mean!! You don't even know what you're talking about. You NEVER let me watch shows I like. Every other kid I know gets to watch that show except for me!"

And on it goes. Daisy ends up storming off to her room, kicking her little brother's Lego castle on her way. Now *he's* frustrated.

Note: When a child is frustrated, *it's not a good time to teach, advise, or lecture.* A child cannot process what you're saying when he's upset, and the onslaught of words you deliver to try to convince him to see things a different way just aggravates him more. Think of it this way: Language is a function of the left brain, and feelings originate in the right. When a child is stuck in the maelstrom of emotions whirling around in his right brain, he doesn't have access to his verbal, logical left brain, which might be able to make sense of or benefit from your well-meaning suggestions. In a sense, your efforts to cool him down by offering rational input is like knocking on their left brain when nobody's home, leaving him feeling alone in the storm of his feelings.

> When a child is frustrated, it's not a good time to teach, advise, or lecture.

Often, as a child's emotions start escalating, the parent tends to either get upset right along with him or use logic to talk him out of his feelings, with terrible results. If you engage in heated negotiations that involve having to explain to your child why he can't have or do what he wants, you're no longer in charge.

No one is in charge: "The Two Lawyers"

This is the equivalent of two lawyers engaged in a heated debate, each trying to sway the other to his point of view. Talking things over may be appropriate and even necessary later when things have calmed down, but not while your child is angry. Being in charge means you're comfortable with the decision you've made and are capable of joining him as he moves through his anger and adjusts to the reality of your decision.

VERSION 3: Mom attempts to move the universe to line up with what Daisy wants.

Daisy: "So, can I watch that show, Mom? Please? PLEASE?!"

Mom: "Well . . . I don't really think it's a good idea, honey. It doesn't finish till pretty late."

Daisy: "C'mon, Mom. Why can't I watch it? Every single person I know is watching it!"

Mom: "All right, I guess it's okay."

Daisy: "Great! Love you, Mom! You're the best!"

Fast-forward to the next morning: Daisy had trouble falling asleep after watching the show. She just had to text her friends for half an hour to talk about the program and ended up falling asleep about an hour later than usual, resulting in a very slow-starting, cranky wake-up the next morning, no real breakfast, and bickering between mother and daughter all the way to school.

Mom: "That's the *last time* I let you watch that show, Daisy. See?! This is what I told you always happens!"

Daisy: "I hate you!!"

Daisy has not learned to adapt; and inevitably, Mom—who herself needs to hit the Wall of Futility as it pertains to thinking her daughter will love and appreciate her more if she gives in to what she wants—is feeling aggressive, angry, and hurt! Using the two-fisted model, the left hand (representing the child) was *above* the right hand (the parent) in this scenario. The child was in charge, and things quickly fell apart.

Child is in charge

VERSION 4: Mom, in charge, walks Daisy to the Wall of Futility.

Mom: "I know you want to watch the show, honey. I can see that it's something you were really hoping you'd get to do."

Daisy: "It WAS . . . it IS! And I *should* be able to! Everybody else at my entire school gets to watch that show but me!"

Mom: "Oh, sweetie . . . what a tough thing it is to feel like you're the only one."

Daisy: "Whatever. I hate you."

Mom: "I understand you'd be pretty mad at me for not letting you do something you want to do so badly."

Daisy: "You have no idea how furious I am. It's so stupid that you're so strict. You treat me like a baby."

Mom: "I guess it stinks when I don't treat you the way you want me to."

Daisy: "No kidding. You have no idea how angry you make me."

Mom: "I'm sorry you're so frustrated. . . ." *[Mom just sits by Daisy quietly, unrushed and present, giving Daisy the space to feel what she's feeling without trying to fix it or talk her out of what she's going through.]* "Do you want to tell me more? Does it seem like I do this a lot—keep you from doing things you want to do?"

Daisy: *[after being quiet and sulky for a while, but very aware that Mom's still there]* "You just treat me so much like a baby, Mom. You don't let me stay up late; you don't let me wear a lot of outfits that a lot of other kids get to wear. You make me feel like I'm five years old or something."

Mom: "It's got to be hard for you to feel so stuck—especially if you feel like you're not getting to do so many things that matter so much to you." [*Notice that Mom can say these things without necessarily agreeing with Daisy's perception, or turning the conversation into a lecture or explanation of why she parents Daisy the way she does.*]

Daisy: "I hate my life."

Mom: [*who is still just sitting beside Daisy being quietly present*] "I'm sorry, honey. I'm so, so sorry that things are hard for you."

Daisy: [*snuffling a little*] "I just hate everything." [*Daisy is moving from Anger and Bargaining to Depression, or sadness.*]

Mom: "Honey . . ."

Daisy: [*starts to cry, leans into Mom; she has hit the Wall.*]

Mom: "We'll get through this, sweetie. I'm here, and we'll figure it out. . . ."

Mom quietly comforts her daughter without saying a whole lot, but staying with Daisy until the storm passes.

Parent is in charge

The next day Daisy's mood is surprisingly lighter and happier, and she seems especially open to her mom.

In the last scenario, Mom doesn't waiver, nor does she worry that Daisy might not like her. She doesn't engage in a discussion about the Neck Up, content portion of what Daisy is saying. But she isn't bossy or tyrannical, either. She's simply and confidently handling the situation, making what she considers to be the best decisions on her daughter's behalf. She helps her daughter really *grasp* that she's not going to be able to watch the show, and when Daisy feels the depth of her own sadness and is encouraged to express it without Mom lecturing or rationalizing her out of her feelings, she's able to move on. *She has adapted* and has come to Acceptance.

Note: Hysterical crying or crocodile tears are not the same as *sadness*. A preteen girl who has been rejected by her friends might express her aggression by sending them scathing emails or chasing after them to convince them to "take her back," but she has not yet hit her Wall of Futility and is stuck in the Bargaining phase of her grief. Similarly, a child who knows how to turn on the faucet, so to speak, and produce tears to get his way hasn't hit the Wall either. Just as an alcoholic needs to hit bottom before being able to start taking steps towards a new, healthier direction, a child needs to fully feel his sadness in order to move towards growing up; and who better to hold his hand while he experiences his grief than a loving parent?

An indication that a child is moving towards acceptance is when she shifts from saying things like "If Franny and Zoe are there, I refuse to go to Casey's birthday even if she *is* my best friend, and you can't make me!" to something softer like, "I wish I didn't have to go. . . ." Parents can model their own process of coming to grips with a disappointment: "I'm sad, too, sweetheart, that you're hurting. I sure wish we could make those girls be nicer to you," rather than "Here's what I think you should do. . . ." (For more on this, see Chapter 6.)

The importance of children learning to handle disappointment

When we inhabit the role of being captain of the ship in our children's lives, we embrace the idea that there's value in helping them chalk up another adaptation, knowing that each time they do, they're adding to the internal reservoir of confidence and resourcefulness that will help them navigate life's ups and downs.

As parents, we often miss the forest for the trees, wanting our kids to be—or at least appear to be—happy in the moment, without considering the cost. When our children grow up believing that they can only *really* be happy if events in their lives unfold in the particular way they want them to, they become handicapped adults, unable to cope with experiences outside their control, and suffering as a result. Parents who help their youngsters learn the essential life skill of adaptation have bestowed upon them a priceless gift, equipping them with the means to be happy regardless of whether people, events, or circumstances conform to their expectations.

Not long ago my son was urged to attend an extended-family member's birthday party on the very last day of the school year. I was aware that he and his buddies had lined up something fun to do but I stayed out of it, leaving the decision about attending the party up to him. He decided to go to the birthday, and when we passed some of his friends who were on their way to an end-of-school celebration, I asked him if he was okay with not hanging out with his buddies. "There'll be other times, Mom. I'm cool." It was as simple as that. The kid had surpassed his Mom (that would be me) in his ability to slip right into adaptation. He insists on enjoying his life and has chosen not to "sweat the small stuff."

When we raise kids by modeling our own adaptation and help them "hit the wall" when they're stuck, we equip them with the ability to surf the waves of life's ups and downs with their eye on the prize: enjoying each day and every moment of their precious lives.

Questions and Suggestions

Question: *"When my son can't have another cookie or story, he blows his stack. I've tried explaining to him that he's only going to get one cookie, and I pretty much stick to that. But he still has a fit. What should I do to help him adapt?"*

Suggestion: First, make sure *you're* not being triggered; and if you are, deal with your own reactions before trying to help him settle down. (See Chapter 1.) Calmly and confidently let your little boy know that you can see how upset he is by not getting another cookie or story; acknowledge how much he wants it, and how sad or mad he is (or both) that he's not getting something that he wants so badly. Help put into words what he seems to be feeling. Be his interpreter. Don't lecture him or try to explain why he can't have it; *this is not a teachable moment.*

Instead, continue offering him your understanding. You might even get a little misty around the eyes yourself, priming his tears. "You wanted that cookie so badly you could almost taste it, didn't you lovey? It's hard to not get something you want so much." If you handle his frustration this way, he should respond by leaning into you, feeling his sadness, and—with a child that young—he'll most likely cry and move on.

Kids being kids, they're naturally going to ask for more of whatever's good, regardless of how often they've been told they can't have it. So, rather than getting hot and bothered about why they keep pushing for what they've been told they aren't allowed to have, relax and come *alongside* them as they do yet another round in the dance of learning how to adapt.

And by the way, there may be times when it actually would be fine for him to have the second cookie or when you're simply too weary to stand your ground. If that's the case, you can still hold your place as being in charge by simply saying, *"You must have read my mind! I was just about to offer you a second cookie!"* This preserves your role as Captain of the ship, and also avoids a meltdown you are too exhausted to face. Make sure you only do this, however, if the child is still being polite, so you aren't rewarding him for having a cookie tantrum.

Question: *"My nine-year-old son falls apart when he's angry. If I have to change plans and can't take him to the movies as I'd hoped or if he finds out we're out of his favorite ice cream, he follows me around the house, insisting I explain to him why he can't have what he wants, even after I've given him reasons. He's usually not one to cry, as you've suggested here. How can I help him to just accept it when things don't go his way?"*

Suggestion: It sounds as though a few things are going on. The first piece to this question has to do with you managing your own reactions. I would urge you to turn around a statement like *"My son should accept it when things don't go his way"* or *"My son shouldn't follow me around when he can't have what he wants."* Look for reasons why the *opposite* of those thoughts might be just as true as your reasoning, or possibly even truer (*"My son should* not *accept it when things go his way" or "My son* should *follow me around when he can't have what he wants").*

It might help you to consider that his ability to behave a particular way when he's disappointed may be more challenging than you realize. Some children have what I call "sticky brain." Dr. Daniel Amen[2] is a psychiatrist whose use of Spect scans has enabled us to get a look at the brain, and there appears to be a correlation between an overactive area called the cingulated gyrus and inflexible, obsessive behaviors in children and adults. I'm by no means suggesting this is in fact what causes your son's difficulty in letting things go; but regardless, you want to strive to be less triggered when he gets upset so that you can show up as the one in charge who can help him feel his sadness and move on.

Start by making sure that when he does melt down or follow you around, you don't end up caving in. Although I don't believe it's possible for parents to *consistently* be consistent, in cases like yours it's especially confusing to a youngster if nagging and whining sometimes lead to them getting what they want. I would urge you to *not* participate in discussions, debates, and negotiations while he's upset. He won't really be hearing you, and it's doubtful that he'll be satisfied by your explanations, regardless of how logical they are.

Instead, hold on to your calm and kindness, and let him know you're aware of how badly he wanted to see that movie or how much he loves that ice cream. Use a BIG, FAT PERIOD at the end of your sentence rather than rambling on about why he can't have what he wants. Speak with authority. For many children, the best tactic is to avoid saying much, and to instead simply sit still and giving them the space they need to be angry and upset. Don't try to talk your son out of his feelings or be in a hurry for him to move on. You may want to have a punching bag or a paper bag stuffed with newspapers hung from a tree outside where he can go at it and get out his frustrations. If you have something to do, go and do it. Eventually your goal is the same as it was for the five-year-old: to help him find and feel his sadness and move on to adaptation.

Later, when things are calm, you may talk with him about what it's like for him to have such a hard time with the outside world not matching his expectations. Sometimes I use the image of comparing an imaginary snapshot in our hand of what we *want* a situation to look like with the actual situation as it is. "What was that like for you today, when you wanted the ice cream so badly and couldn't have it?" By creating a safe, nonjudgmental space for him to offload his frustration, you are building the connection between the two of you and reducing the buildup of frustration he may be carrying. (Read more about this in Chapter 6.)

***

Question: *"My seven-year-old son loves building things with Legos; but if he can't get a part to go on right, he becomes almost violent, throwing pieces across the room and refusing to clean up after himself. Sometimes I tell him I'm going to take the Legos away if he doesn't handle his temper better, and he promises to be good, but he usually loses it at some point. His anger upsets our whole family! What's wrong with him?"*

Suggestion: At the risk of appearing to be a one-trick pony, I would suggest you begin dealing with this issue by focusing on the place where you have the most influence: your own reactions. If you were in my office for a session, I would ask you to look at the thoughts you've had concerning your son that are expressed in your question: "*My son shouldn't lose his temper when he's frustrated,*" and "*My son should stop playing Legos when he's having a hard time.*" What are some reasons that he *should* lose his temper when he's frustrated? If he has no other resources for dealing with things when they don't go his way, it would make perfect sense for him to lose his temper!

If you go through the process of looking at the stories and beliefs that get you triggered, you may find yourself coming up with turnarounds like "*I shouldn't lose my temper when I get upset*" (if you're human, you probably have) or "*I should stop doing _____ when I'm having a hard time dealing with it.*" (Fill in the blank with whatever it is that you push yourself to do even when you're out of patience.)

Once you've taken some of the finger pointing and judgment out of the mix, you'll be in a much better place to help your son deal with his own short fuse. Remember, *while* he's upset is not the time to try to teach, advise, or enlighten him. A child in the midst of a meltdown is deaf; he is simply incapable of hearing or processing whatever wise counsel you may offer.

Instead, mirror back to him what he's feeling. "Oh sweetheart, you've been trying so hard to get that one section to look the way you wanted." Give him room to feel what he feels. Offer kindness and warmth. If he'll let you, take him in your arms. Again, your goal is to walk him to the Wall of Futility and help him feel his sadness and find his tears so that he can move on.

It's important to be aware that children who are *chronically* frustrated—who are in a sense trigger-happy with their rage—need to visit the Wall of Futility a number of times to begin to soften so they get used to feeling their frustration and moving through it. These kinds of kids—and I see them quite often—walk around with what I call a low-grade fever of frustration. It takes very little to set them off, because they're nearly always feeling agitated internally. By helping them with Act I (Chapter 6), by staying deeply connected while holding your place as the Captain of the ship, and by walking them through their sadness when disappointed (instead of rationally trying to explain why they can't have what they want) you'll help diffuse chronic frustration at its root.

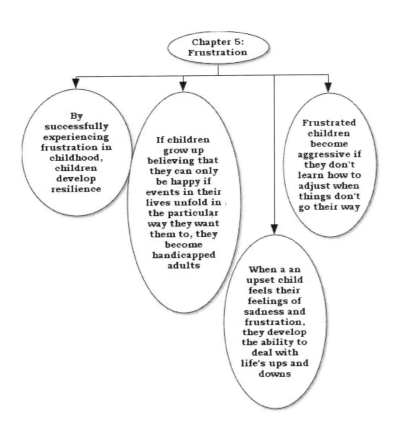

Chapter Six
Handling Resistance, Anger, Whining, Meltdowns, and Aggression
"We need soft hearts to grow up."
Gordon Neufeld

The most frequent calls for help that I get are from parents whose kids who are aggressive, have frequent meltdowns, or whose family members feel they have to walk on eggshells to avoid triggering their explosions. I coach these parents to fortify the foundation of attachment and regain their role as captain of the ship for their child. I also teach them how to help their youngster deal with the nearly constant state of frustration that runs like a low-grade fever, predisposing her to become agitated. I refer them to material that helps them better understand their child's brain and how it might be influencing her behavior (as well as their own). But sometimes, more is needed.

Act I and Act II: *What is it like to be you?*
There are two stages involved in the process of working with a child whose behavior is problematic. The first, which I refer to as **Act I**, has to do with providing a troubled child with the opportunity to offload her upset. The key phrases I ask parents to keep in mind as they're interacting with their child are "What is it like to be you?" and "Tell me more."

The goal of Act I is to allow the child to express the "neck down" portion of her experience. While I don't expect youngsters to accurately put into words the reasons for their anger or resistance, I have come to understand that it is essential to allow hurting children to feel heard. I ask parents to refrain from offering advice, suggestions, information, or insights during Act I. If a child has adequately offloaded and expressed her emotions and feels understood during Act I, she is more naturally likely to be *receptive* to what you have to say in Act II. Still, I suggest that parents *ask* the child, after Act I, whether she would now be willing to hear some of their thoughts or ideas. If the child says no, I urge parents to drop the matter for the moment. Generally speaking, once a child has said her piece, she will feel open to hearing what her parents have to say.

Note: Act I questions are simply designed to keep the child talking. Sometimes your comment will just be an expression of dismay, designed to communicate your compassion and care. "How did that make you feel?" is *not* an Act I question, and tends to shut children down. Most kids don't accurately know what they feel, and this question feels like you're trying to talk like a therapist. Simply ask questions or make noises that motivate your child to keep expressing their upset.

Act I questions or comments	Act II Questions or comments
"What was that like for you?"	"Maybe we can try invite Danny, instead..."
"It sounds like that was pretty tough to take..."	"I'm not sure she meant to hurt you..."
"Oh, sweetie..."	"We You could record that the show and watch it later..."
"*That's* a very big feeling..."	"I wonder if there's someone else who can come over to play..."
"It's hard when you can't have what you want so badly..."	"I'm not sure your teacher really doesn't really hopes you'll flunk..."

Use Act I comments, questions or appropriate sound effects ("Oh sweetheart!", "Mmph!) until your child has settled down. If you skip to forcefully offering suggestions or advice (Act II), he won't really hear or process what you're saying. I call that "crashing the party." Remember, when you *need* a child to feel better, in essence you're abdicating your captain of the ship role and shifting the dynamic so their hand is above yours. Take your time with Act I and avoid rushing to Act II.

One image that I use is the way the hair on a dog stands up when he first sees a stranger approach. Most of us have learned not to push ourselves on a dog that's in an agitated state. Instead, we watch for his ears to lie down, his tail to start wagging and the hairs on his back to lay flat again. This is the sort of thing to watch for that will suggest a child is ready for your input, advice or information (Act II.)

A key phrase I ask parents to keep in mind as they're interacting with their child is "What is it like to be you?"

An angry young man

Cheryl and Dane walked through my door with their son, a sullen looking fifteen-year-old boy. Jason barely looked at me as he entered, and he made sure his parents caught a glimpse of his scowl as he sat down in my office. Dane started right in with a litany of what he considered to be his son's problems, flaws, and mistakes. I was told that Jason was "a very smart boy" who "makes trouble wherever he goes." Cheryl chimed in, "He constantly torments his younger brother and sister. He absolutely will not leave them alone. If we try to get him to stop, he rages at us. If we're lucky, he stomps off to his room, slams the door, and hides out in there for the rest of the night."

Child is in charge

Dane finished for his wife. "When we're not so lucky, something in the house gets broken. Or one of the little kids gets hurt. When we ask Jason what he's so angry about, he can't seem to come up with a reason that explains all this rage. He complains that we favor the little kids, or that we don't do enough for him, which is crazy! We've had it!"

I watched Jason as his parents listed his many transgressions. Subtle as it was, I couldn't help but see him wince as they went on and on. Truth be told, I was cringing myself as I listened to the intensity of his parents' accusations and the absence of any warmth in their voice. As I watched this family in the first few moments of our session, I was struck by how much each of them needed understanding, connection, and simple kindness. Jason had never really had an Act I; his parents lived in an Act II world, constantly scolding, criticizing, and lecturing their son. Given the fact that he didn't feel seen or understood by his mom and dad, he was completely unreceptive to them.

Jason's parents went on to tell me that nothing they tried seemed to work with him. "We've taken away his video games, we've grounded him, and we've even made him do extra chores. It doesn't matter what we do—he just says, 'Whatever,' and continues to be impossible."

Usually, my goal in working with a family is to coach the parents to strengthen their attachment with their child and learn to manage their own reactions so that *they* can be the calm, confident captains of the ship for their child. I help parents foster a connection with their kids that will awaken their natural instincts to cooperate. But in this family's case I worked not only with Cheryl and Dane but also privately with their son for a couple of months. Jason was in immediate need of a safe place to vent his feelings without having them minimized or dismissed, and he desperately needed a healthy adult connection. His parents were too entrenched in their views of Jason as The Problem to provide him with the support he needed.

In my sessions with this young man, I soon found out that he was a very sensitive young man who had lost his way. Problems with friends, schoolwork, and ongoing tension with his parents had created stress that he was simply incapable of dealing with. In addition, over the course of our work it became evident that Jason had some ADHD symptoms—distractibility, impulse problems, low frustration tolerance, and a hair-trigger reactivity—which, thrown in with the hormones of adolescence, made him prone to chronic irritability, sullenness, and rage.

I started my work with Dane and Cheryl by creating what I felt to be the most fundamental change called for: helping them manage the negative, shaming beliefs that triggered their unproductive and hurtful reactions to Jason's misbehavior. I pointed out that when they believed thoughts like *Jason should appreciate the things we do for him,* or *Jason should be nicer to his little brother and sister,* they headed down the road to ruin—a road that inevitably led to losing their cool, threatening, and creating drama in the household that simply hardened Jason's heart and made him more resistant to their input. Before they could hope to have Jason be receptive to them, they were going to need to deal with the upsetting thoughts that were triggering their own reactivity, which—like a domino effect—ended up further alienating their son and eliminating any hope that he would be responsive to their guidance and input.

Once Dane and Cheryl realized that I wasn't judging or grading them on their parenting, they became open to looking honestly at their conflicts with Jason. When they understood the difference between coming *at* their son versus coming *alongside* him, they began to see the world through his eyes. This softened them considerably.

"I can see a lot of reasons why Jason *shouldn't* be nicer to the younger kids. They annoy him, they mess with his stuff, and we tend to favor them because—frankly—they're a whole lot easier to be around," Dane told me. "But now that I understand all these other things Jason's struggling with—at school and with his friends—I can see how the little kids would be a logical outlet for his stress. I'm not saying I approve or anything, but I can see how it makes its own kind of sense."

By lessening their judgments of Jason, his parents were positioning themselves to approach him in a way that had a far greater chance of producing a more favorable outcome. As they worked to get out from under the grip of their negative stories and judgments about their son, they were better able to avoid engaging in a power struggle with him, which they already knew brought about resistance and anger.

As Cheryl and Dane moved from judging to understanding Jason, they became genuinely interested in restoring an authentic connection with him, and began working the stages of attachment (see Chapter 2.) Cheryl was stunned one day when Jason agreed to make cookies with her when everyone else was out of the house. "Normally, I'm the last person he'd want to spend time with. But we had a good time together. And he loved it that I didn't make him save cookies for his dad or siblings. I was actually a little sad when everyone else came home. I felt like I had some time with the Jason I used to know—like he had peeked out from under his shell. It was great!"

Dane made a special effort to ask Jason to help him rearrange the living room furniture. The two of them had what he later said was one of the best times together he could remember having in the last couple of years. They argued about what to put where; but as he related the story to me, he said, "It was fun!

And I didn't feel like I had to always give in to what Jason wanted. I have to say, a lot of times he had a really creative idea that I got excited about, and I could tell he was jazzed. After that night, it seemed like things started to get better. I found myself looking for little things for the two of us to do together, even for a few minutes."

In my sessions with Jason, I focused mostly on creating enough trust between us so that he would be willing to let me know some of the things he was dealing with that he didn't yet feel comfortable sharing with his parents, including the fact that some of the boys at school had been calling him a loser, and teasing him about his inferior athletic ability. When I asked him if he'd told his folks, he replied, "All they ever do when I tell them I'm having trouble with something is to give me advice or explain why it's my fault."

I asked him what he would say to his parents if he knew they would truly hear him, without interrupting or advising. He poured forth a list of things he longed to be able to tell them. I was both deeply struck by how much this young man had been trying to deal with on his own, and how desperately in need he was of his parents' loving support. As our connection solidified and his parents were doing their part to reclaim their parental role in Jason's life, Jason allowed me to tell his parents about what was going on with the kids at school. I had some poignant sessions with them together in which Jason cautiously revealed more of the truth about the hard times he'd been going through over the last few months. With a bit of coaching, his parents did what parents do best: They listened with compassion and love and helped their son lean on them as the captains of the ship and stalwart supporters he so needed them to be.

It wasn't an easy journey, and there were times when Jason raged, but within a relatively short time, he and his parents had forged a healthier and more honest connection. As Dane and Cheryl became more willing to see Jason *as is*, with his challenges as well as his gifts, they awakened a new level of receptivity in him to respond to their direction and receive their much needed support and guidance.

The three yeses

When someone is upset, even though we might think they want the other person to agree with them, the truth is, they just want to be heard and understood. In one of our sessions I had Jason and his parents play a game I call "The Three Yeses." I instructed Jason to face his mom and to talk for about two minutes about whatever might be upsetting him. Cheryl's job was to simply listen to her son with a quiet mind, without preparing a rebuttal, interrupting, or rolling her eyes. At the end of the two minutes I told Cheryl I wanted her to rephrase three things her son had told her in such a way as to prompt him to say, "Yes." Then I explained, "If Jason said, 'I don't like it when you take away my video games for no good reason,' then Cheryl, you wouldn't start lecturing him about why they've been taken away. You would simply say, 'One thing I heard you say, Jason, is that you don't like it when I take away your video games, and you don't feel there's a good reason.'"

Jason and Cheryl followed my directions, and after she got her three "yeses" from Jason, it was Cheryl's turn to speak for two minutes while Jason listened. This family seemed to breathe a collective sigh of relief as they have the chance to feel truly heard by the others. Dane and Cheryl later told me they ended up using this approach at home not only with their kids but also with one another, with great results.

I asked Cheryl and Dane to consider the difference between throwing seeds on dry, rocky earth and throwing seeds on cultivated, healthy soil. "You can throw thousands of seeds on dry, uncultivated ground, but the seeds won't have much chance of sprouting. Similarly, if we want our kids to be receptive to our support and direction, we first need to create a natural openness in them by helping them feel heard and by giving them the sense that we're unquestionably on their side."

> If we want our kids to be receptive to our support and direction, we first need to create a natural receptivity in them by helping them feel unquestionably that we're on their side.

Dane told me, "Looking back at his explosiveness and resistance from this new perspective—seeing it more as a symptom of other things he was struggling with—I almost can't imagine how he *wouldn't* be difficult and angry most of the time." His mom let me know they had made some adjustments to ensure a better diet and more sleep, which she said helped his mood. "We're also scheduled to meet with the school and talk about maybe doing some testing for ADD. But meanwhile, we've met with his teacher and she's been great about giving Jason a little extra help now that she knows he's been struggling and isn't just apathetic."

When children or teens are chronically frustrated and have no outlet, their pent-up feelings fuel a constant, low-grade irritability. If these kids have circumstantial stressors—competition with siblings, impatient parents, ongoing academic challenges, or peer problems—they're primed to become easily upset. Throw in neurological disregulation and/or hormones, as they move through adolescence, and it becomes clear that without help from caring adults, it's nearly impossible for them not to become explosive when push comes to shove. These are the younger kids who have frequent meltdowns and tantrums, or the older ones who become sullen, withdrawn, or full of rage. I sometimes call these rages a result of *straw-that-broke-the-camel's-back syndrome.* If a child is overloaded with stress or frustration, it may take next to nothing to set him off. Unless the parents look at the situation from the bigger picture, they'll focus on the irrationality of their child's explosion based on whatever little thing seemingly provoked it. But the truth is, it wasn't the little thing, it was the accumulation of too many huge emotions swirling around inside, with no outlet.

When a parent comes *at* a child like this and issues ever-escalating threats or criticism, the situation only gets worse. Psychologists have coined the term "dry-eyed syndrome" to describe kids who are hardened, detached, and uncaring. Regardless of how we punish these kids or what we take away that they care about, they will not soften, feel their sadness, or find their tears, and therefore cannot find their way to adaptation.

When parents consistently respond to their child's communications from the neck up, the child feels misunderstood, which then fuels her ongoing sense of frustration. Consistently focusing on a youngster's words and ignoring the emotions underneath adds fuel to the fire of a child's anger. The child has the experience of her feelings being minimized or diminished, and she responds with her own efforts to logically argue her case. Using the two-fists analogy introduced in Chapter 1, this scenario would be represented by the "parent" fist and the "child" fist being side by side. No one is in charge, and each side is attempting to use logic to convince the other of the rightness of her perception and point of view—"The Two Lawyers."

No one is in charge: "The Two Lawyers"

Conversely, when Mom or Dad help translate for an angry child what she's experiencing, they help her discover the way back to herself and thus successfully adapt to life's disappointments.

In the past, when Cheryl and Dane asked Jason why he was angry, he would tell them it was because they always favored his two younger siblings. His parents typically responded from the neck up, telling Jason that he was being ridiculous and giving him examples of all the times when he had gotten his way despite the protests of his younger brother and sister. Therefore, he took his rage underground, which explains how his parents had contributed to the volcano that frequently erupted in their household.

More often than we realize, even if our youngsters or teens tell us why they're angry, the answer they give isn't accurate. Even we adults get it wrong, thinking we're upset because someone took our parking place when we're really mad because the plumbing backed up and the plumber refused to come until the next day. We are often tricked by our children's sophisticated mastery of language; this is particularly true of the kids who have a wide repertoire of "feeling words." We need to be careful not to give inappropriate weight to the answers our children offer when they're trying to explain why they're upset.

Our challenge as parents is to interpret for our kids what we sense is contributing to their anger. We need to try to speak on behalf of the fury underneath our children's words or behavior. As we learned earlier, this sometimes means gently guiding children to the Wall of Futility when they're frustrated, so they can offload their feelings of discouragement or disappointment and move on to adaptation. In this spirit, parents see their children's behavior—or misbehavior—as an *announcement*, and they rise to the challenge to find the true message being expressed. Like Sherlock Holmes, parents use clues to decode what their children are truly saying with their words and behavior.

"What color are you feeling?"
One of the ways I help children connect to their emotions is to ask them to imagine feelings as having colors. I might suggest we use red for anger, yellow for worry, black for sad, orange for happiness and so on. If a child is telling me something upsetting, I'll say, "What colors are swirling around in you now?" If she tells me there are a lot of red (anger) and black (sad) feelings, I encourage her to point to the part of the body where those feelings are happening. "Is it mostly black, or mostly red? Is there any orange in there?" This is an excellent way to help some children stay in their bodies and move through their emotions rather than disconnect and intellectualize when they're distressed.

Had Jason's parents attempted to get *underneath* his words, they might have responded to his comment about them preferring his siblings by saying, "It sounds like you feel that your brother and sister have it easier than you." By sending Jason the clear message that they wanted to understand what he was feeling, rather than win an argument, they would have helped him feel heard and understood, which would have greatly decreased the fuel that so frequently set this young boy's anger ablaze.

Parent is in charge

Aggressive for no apparent reason

Many times, parents or teachers come to see me because their children are aggressive toward others, seemingly without cause. Suzanne was a veteran teacher who came to me for advice about a particularly troublesome second grade student. "I've been doing this for nearly thirty years and have all kinds of tricks up my sleeve, but this kid has me stumped. I'm worn out by him!" Jarrod had a history of hitting and pushing that dated back to kindergarten, but recently he had become much more aggressive towards his classmates. His most recent infraction involved him walking from the classroom to the playground at recess and, without provocation, promptly pushing over a smaller child.

I asked Suzanne to shift her thinking from considering what she should have done *after* he pushed the child over— "What should I have done to stop him from doing these sorts of things?"—to considering what made it *logical* that he would walk onto the playground and push a child over. "Why would it make perfect sense for Jarrod to knock over that child? Put your inner lawyer aside for a minute—the one who has a long list of reasons why his behavior was unacceptable—and pull the camera back to see this aggression in context. What was going in Jarrod that made pushing that child almost inevitable?"

Suzanne told me that Jarrod's mom had let her know there was significant marital tension and conflict in the home; she also made it clear that she was too overwhelmed with the problems in her own life to do much about how Jarrod was coping. In addition, she said it was nearly impossible to get her sleepy son out of the house in time for her to drop him at school and make it to work, so she packed his "breakfast" (usually a sugary juice drink, donut and apple) in his lunchbox for him to eat before school began. Jarrod normally arrived about twenty minutes before class started and roamed the playground, usually playing with older boys who were very competitive.

Once class began, Jarrod was generally fidgety and unfocused, practically leaping out of his chair when the bell rang for recess. On the day of his most recent offense, as soon as class was dismissed to go outside, Jarrod walked out to the playground and promptly pushed over an unsuspecting child.

I told Suzanne my first impressions. "First, you clearly have a child who's hurting emotionally. If there's tension between his parents, Jarrod feels it. A child's behavior—or misbehavior—can be a remarkable barometer for the 'climate' in a family. His mom has admitted to being unable to help him sort out his distress, which means he needs another caring adult in his "village" to lean on right now."

"On top of that, it sounds like Jarrod has a history of poor impulse control. Throw in fatigue, frustration (from playing with the older boys), the absence of a good breakfast to help him feel grounded, plus fruit and fruit juice—sugar and more sugar— and you have a child with *no* self-control. Chances are, it happened so fast that he probably doesn't even know why he pushed that child over."

Suzanne told me that when she had asked Jarrod why he'd done it, he had in fact replied, "I don't know. I pushed him before I could stop myself."

I asked her to consider some proactive measures she could take in the future to *prevent* Jarrod's aggression. She said, "I could spend some time with him before school when things in my room are quiet. As much as I could use that time to prepare for the day, it would actually make my job easier if Jarrod could get some of the anger and hurt off his chest by talking with me. I think it would help him if I just listened and showed him that I care, even though I'll also see if I can arrange for him to visit with the school counselor.

"Jarrod almost always gets frustrated when he plays with those older boys before school. I can speak to the playground teacher about helping him find a structured game or a situation with kids where he doesn't feel he has to prove himself. By the time he walks into the classroom door at 8:15 he's already wound up and agitated when he's been playing with the tougher boys.

"Since I know Jarrod has had an especially hard time managing his aggression, I could give him a job of some kind to do at recess. He loves feeling important, and I think having a special task would help him stay on track. And I know how he gets when he's had sweets on an empty stomach. I can ask his mom to consider packing him with something more nutritious."

Suzanne sent me an email a few days later saying that she had implemented some of these ideas and things had improved already. She said she loved how empowering it was to look backwards from problem situations to rethink how they could be avoided, rather than focusing on how to come up with better punishments or consequences for children once they had gotten in trouble. I replied by saying, "This is what ship captains do: They scan the horizon for potential problems so they can steer clear of them."

When a child is chronically aggressive, it's important to rule out biological, emotional and neurological contributors. But whether or not these factors contribute to the problem, an angry child still needs a caring adult to help him articulate his emotions and feel understood. Rather than focusing on how to respond *after* his misbehavior, when caretakers seek to offload a child's daily frustrations by listening and helping him get to the Wall of Futility, they drain the fuel from the tank that perpetually feeds his rage. In Jarrod's case, I also urged Suzanne to see if she could encourage his mother to consider how unsettled he was by the conflict at home and offer her some counseling referrals. In addition, having a better diet and more structure at playtime provided this young man with the external support that helped him be more successful.

What is the payoff for this misbehavior?
It's important to consider the payoff a child is receiving for her problematic behavior. I call this "playing the captain of the ship game." It involves considering how the child's misbehavior makes its own kind of sense.

Ellen came to see me because her six-year-old daughter, Lara, whined incessantly. In this case, the captain of the ship will ask, "If whining is the answer, what is the question? (This works a bit like the game *Jeopardy*.) Instead of resisting the whining—which simply promotes more of it—how can we consider the ways Lara's whining might make sense? What would Lara have to be experiencing or feeling to behave this way? How is it serving her?"

I helped Ellen take two steps back from her irritation and step into a more detached, *curious* vantage point about her daughter's behavior. Ellen came up with a number of good reasons why Lara *should* whine—as strange as that sounded. "It helps her feel like the baby of the family again, a position her younger brother has taken over," she told me. "And it's a surefire way of getting me to engage. Even if I tell Lara, 'I'm going to ignore you if you whine,' she still gets attention from me, even though it's negative."

> If whining is the answer, what is the question?

If a child gets lots of *partial, halfhearted* attention from you most of the time but gets your *undivided* attention when she acts up, chances are she'll act up. It's a bit like choosing between a pound of bland, dehydrated potato flakes or a few bites of a nutritionally loaded protein bar. One is just filler, but the other one satisfies.

I explained to Ellen that if a child can't have half an hour of your time, she'll go for the juiciest, most dramatic, action-packed five minutes she can get. I call this turning on Mom TV. (See more on this in Chapter 7) Either she'll create a scenario where you're heavily engaged in a conflict—which at least means you're satisfying her desire to have all of you—or you, as captain of the ship, can orchestrate a nourishing few minutes, telling jokes, singing a song, or cuddling quietly.

Ellen considered how she could help her daughter have more of her attention in a positive way and how Lara might be given some of the goodies she was missing from when she had been the baby. As Ellen began looking for healthy ways to give Lara what she had been getting by whining, it significantly lessened.

Children who interrupt

Sometimes parents complain that their children interrupt them when they're talking with others. Consider this scenario: Joey interrupts Mom once, and she points her finger and says, "Joey, not now." He waits ten seconds and pulls her sleeve a little more forcefully. Again she replies sternly, "JOEY, I *said* not now!" Thirty seconds later Joey pulls Mom's sleeve yet again and pokes her aggressively in the arm, saying, "MOMMY!" Mom, exasperated, responds, "WHAT IS IT, JOEY?!" What a clever little boy Joey is; he's learned that it takes three times and a poke to get Mommy to stop talking to other people and pay attention to *him!*

If Mommy doesn't end up giving her attention to Joey because of his prodding, and she instead catches him waiting quietly for her—even for two seconds—and *then* she says, "Joey, did you want to tell me something?" she'll help him learn how to get what he wants—Mommy's attention—in a less aggressive way. As the calm captain of the ship, she recognizes the limits of his attention span and doesn't make him wait excessively, guiding him towards learning to manage his need for Mommy with an approach to getting it that's acceptable.

Many parents experience the frustration of their child's radar going off the minute they get on the telephone. The child might have absolutely no interest in Mommy until the phone rings, and suddenly he *has* to ask her something *right now!* The solution I used with my son may work for you: I simply told him that unless it was an emergency, whatever he was asking for that prompted him to try to interrupt me if I was on the phone would automatically get a "No" response from me—and then I followed through if he interrupted me. (This, of course, was presuming that "No" was not what he wanted to hear, which was usually the case!) Granted, a parent of a four-year-old can't reasonably expect him to wait twenty minutes while she gabs with a friend; but within a child's capabilities, a parent does no service to her child when she drops everything because he wants her attention.

At such times, it is critically important for a child to have a calm and loving captain at the helm of the ship. By managing our own reactions, thinking ahead, and keeping an eye on the "weather," we can enjoy smooth sailing and enjoy the journey together.

Questions and Suggestions

Question: *Can you tell me how to play the "captain of the ship game" around my eight-year-old's temper tantrums about homework? He completely falls apart, and eventually so do I.*

Suggestion: The basic idea is that instead of figuring out how to *fix* a problematic situation, you think back to the point at which you could have prevented it from happening, and you resolve to take action at that juncture in future interactions with your child. As much as you naturally want to resolve problems when they're already happening, if you look at the big picture, you'll know that what you learn from this round will help you avoid similar problems down the parenting road. There are a few elements to consider when you're trying to understand how things can fall apart for your child:

- **Hunger**. Is he hungry and tired from running on empty? Or has he had too much sugar (or in some cases not enough protein)? Most kids need to feel rested and nourished to be able to handle stress and stay focused on uninteresting tasks.
- **Difficulty paying attention**. It's difficult, if not impossible, for a child to do a boring homework task when interesting things are going on where she's trying to focus, or if siblings are having fun and she feels left out.
- **Dislike of the teacher**. A child who does not feel liked and appreciated by his teacher does not try to please her. If these feelings are especially strong, the child may go out of his way to *displease* her.
- **Difficulty with the assignment**. Some children struggle to understand concepts introduced in the classroom—either because they don't grasp the material or because they're inattentive—and therefore don't feel confident about doing the related homework.
- **Feeling disconnected from Mom/Dad**. Again, kids who feel a lack of connection with their parents may enjoy the focused attention they get from their parents when they throw a fit, even if it's negative. As you'll read later, I call this *Mom TV*.
- **Being in a supportive setting**. Many children like to do their homework in the presence of other family members,

music, or TV. Others need to be in a quiet room to concentrate and stay focused. As captain of the ship, a parent needs to help figure out the right setting for her child.

- **Time for the task**. Some kids need to do homework shortly after coming home from school. Others need to do it after dinner. Some should do it all at once; others do better when they can work in seven- to ten-minute focused increments.
- **Addiction to drama.** Some households seem to run on chaos and drama. If a child is uninterested in homework and desperate to postpone the dreaded task as long as possible, she'll pitch a fit to avoid the task and get the three-ring circus going.

This is by no means an exhaustive list of possibilities, but you get the idea. By thinking about how things were going *before* your child's meltdown and considering how well he was—or wasn't—positioned to care about the homework assignment and be focused, you'll be in a position to help him succeed.

***

Question: *I sometimes worry about how my son is affected by his sister's frequent explosive behavior. He almost always gives up something or compromises to avoid angering her. How can I help him not be impacted by her?*

Suggestion: When one child in a family goes from zero to sixty in a matter of moments, it has a profound effect on everyone else. Children have far fewer resources to draw upon than adult members of the household, so they can end up being seriously impacted by their siblings' aggression.

First and foremost, I would recommend that you address your daughter's explosiveness. Whether that means a professional evaluation for emotional issues or impulse problems, or the introduction of strategies introduced here, it is essential that one child not be allowed to bully her siblings.

As far as your son goes, I would ask him the all-important question "What is it like for you when your sister starts to have a tantrum?" Then just listen. Don't explain, counsel, or enlighten. Simply give him the space to express his feelings, be angry, complain, and/or cry about his experience. Ask him what colors swirl around in his body when she starts shouting (representing emotions, as discussed earlier). He may start out slowly, suggesting, "It's no big deal" or "I don't mind," but if you hang in there and let him know you're able and willing to hear the truth, he will tell you. Be patient, and have this conversation more than once.

Children deserve to feel safe in their own homes. A youngster who is fearful of his sibling will often mute his voice, minimize his own needs, or tiptoe around the house to avoid setting off a rage. Please help your son feel empowered to speak up on his own behalf by protecting him from his sister and letting him feel heard. Ross Greene has some very good suggestions in his book *The Explosive Child.*

***

Question: *Don't you think it's important to talk things over with your child after he has been aggressive or has had a meltdown?*

Suggestion: Yes and no. If you attempt to debrief too soon after an outburst, a child will simply be defensive or impervious to your input. When a youngster has had a meltdown, there's a lot of adrenalin running through his body. It takes time for his nervous system to settle down enough to actually have a rational conversation. That doesn't mean that your child might not welcome your presence to *help* him settle down and recover. It just means that it is not realistic to immediately have any sort of substantive dialog about what caused the aggressive behavior. It's important to move through Act I before you go on to Act II.

After things have quieted down, it would be entirely appropriate to spend some time with him talking about what happened. Make sure your expectations for the length and depth of the conversation are in synch with the child's chronological/developmental age. Most parents use far too many words to say what would be better said briefly. Rather than flood him with a long, drawn out lecture—which usually sends him wandering off in his mind until you're finished talking—speak briefly and to the point. Your words will have far more impact if you don't ramble on.

Start by clearly expressing your concern about what happened and your resolve to prevent these episodes from repeating. Give your child the chance to feel heard, but don't expect him to logically explain why he behaved as he did. Remember, you can dislike or condemn the behavior but *not* the child.

Let him know about any changes you've decided to institute to prevent future problems. This might be that from now on he needs to have his bath *before* watching TV, or that if he doesn't want his little brother to use his Legos, he'll need to put them in a special place where the younger child can't reach them. It could also be that you urge him to start noticing how it feels in his body when he's *starting* to get frustrated or upset so he can come to you to help him calm down *before* the volcano inside him erupts. "Sweetheart, if you feel your heart start to race or if you get all wound up and mad inside, come to me and I'll help you settle down before you do something you'd feel badly about later." You might refer to the imagery of colors as feelings. Assure your child of your belief that most likely he doesn't enjoy feeling so out of control and that you're going to help him avoid these kinds of events in the future.

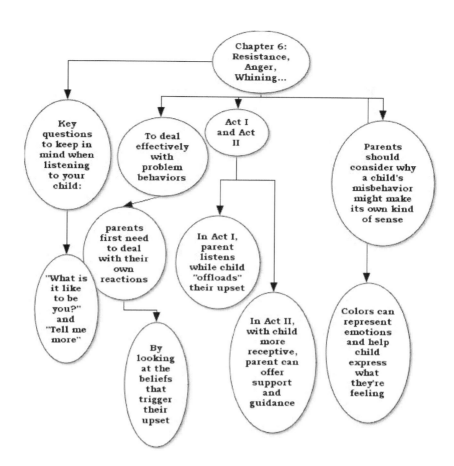

Chapter Seven
How to Get Kids to Cooperate
Newsflash: Kids don't like to be bossed around!

In her infinite wisdom, Mother Nature has designed children to resist being told what to do outside of connection. Kids are wired to *Just say no!* when an outsider attempts to get them to do something, and to only do the bidding of those to whom they are appropriately attached. This makes a lot of sense. Consider what would happen if our children's instincts allowed them to follow and obey people who weren't part of their village. Imagine the worries you would be saddled with if your little ones didn't instinctively refuse the demands of strangers. Momma Nature knew what she was doing when she wired our children's brains to resist being pushed and pulled outside of the context of attachment. So, let's start off with the understanding that, as frustrating as it is when your kids refuse to come to the dinner table or clean up their toys after being asked five times, there are powerful—and invaluable—instincts at work that bias our children towards resistance.

Parent from a loving and secure attachment
There are three primary drives in a human being: fear, frustration, and the need for close and secure attachment. When we understand how primal our children's need is for close connection, we make use of our greatest tool in gaining their cooperation.

The next time your son or daughter voluntarily does what you request, notice how things have been going between the two of you. Chances are, if you turn the clock backwards, you'll find that in one or more ways of attaching, you have been feeding the roots of your connection.

Maybe you spent some special time with your daughter (Proximity) or watched a show on TV you both like (Sameness). Or maybe you stood up for your son in a difficult moment (Belonging/Loyalty) or had a good laugh at one of his jokes (Significance). Perhaps your son caught a glimpse of you watching him quietly with affection (Love), or maybe you simply listened with genuine interest while your daughter told you what she thinks about her math teacher (Being Known). Whatever particular action you took to fortify that loving connection, in all likelihood you had something good going on that predisposed your child to be more cooperative.

If you start paying attention to the times your kids *do* cooperate—as rare as those times might be—you'll discover an important element: Kids cooperate when they feel close to you and when you make a request from a sense of connectedness. When your children or teens do what you ask, you've been tapping into one of their strongest and most primitive requirements: the need for closeness and attachment.

Now, this doesn't mean that you have a poor relationship with your children because you have problems getting them into the car the first time you call them or have trouble convincing them to brush their teeth. Kids are biased towards maximizing their enjoyment of life; they are fully committed to having as much fun as possible in each and every moment. When you ask a child to do something that requires her to give up the good time she's having, she is likely to resist. It works a whole lot better when we accept that reality rather than pretend we don't understand why our kids would rather wrestle on the floor with each other than take a bath and get ready for bed.

The brain matters

In addition, neurology can also contribute to some children's difficulty with being compliant or transitioning from one activity to the next. There are all kinds of ways that wiring influences behavior. For instance, a child with an overactive cingulate (a strip running down the center of the brain) is going to have a more difficult time transitioning and being flexible. You can give this youngster simple instructions, like "Clean up the blocks and put on your PJs," and precipitate a complete meltdown.

A child with slower brain wave activity in the prefrontal cortex is more likely to be forgetful and disorganized. You might ask her to put away her homework, wash her hands, and set the table, and find that your requests didn't register at all or were immediately forgotten. To simply dismiss her as being willful and resistant is to miss potentially important factors that legitimately get in the way of her being cooperative. As little as we know about the brain and its complexities, we are at least beginning to understand that we cannot divorce behavior from neurology.

Regardless of how the brain's wiring contributes to a child's behavior or misbehavior, it remains true that when a child is securely attached to you—meaning he can relax in the awareness that you are his reliable ship captain—he will be more inclined to follow your direction. This is why, rather than viewing a child's oppositional behavior simply as behavior that needs to be shaped by punishments and consequences, it's essential that parents make sure the relationship is in good shape.

> A child who is securely attached to you is far more inclined to follow your direction.

The illusion that force works to improve a child's behavior

Not long ago I watched a television show in which a nanny was brought in to help a completely befuddled and overwhelmed single father who was in desperate need of learning how to parent his two out-of-control boys. While there were some sweet moments—primarily with the nanny providing some much-needed words of kindness to this weary dad—her approach, in my opinion, missed the mark in a number of essential ways.

With the older child—who played about six hours of video games a day, except when he was slugging his brother—the nanny introduced a behavior modification program whereby he lost five minutes of video gaming for each transgression. For the five-year-old (one of the most angry and hurting little boys I'd ever seen), she instituted a "cool down" area where he had to sit if (when) he started a violent outburst with his brother or his father. (Yes, he routinely kicked, hit, and bit his father. The nanny's advice to the father after the child bit him while Dad was trying to restrain his little boy was, "Hold him up higher; that way he can't reach your arm to bite it.")

The little boy was a hurricane of rage when his dad tried to get him to sit in the "cool down" chair, where he was expected to think about what he'd done (not likely). After being carried back to the "cool down" chair by his Dad about thirty-seven times—kicking and screaming—the child finally remained there out of sheer exhaustion. The nanny and father shared a moment savoring this "success." The father had finally overpowered his son.

This is not how you get a child to cooperate. More importantly, it doesn't come close to addressing the elements that prompt a child to misbehave and feel out of control. Dad needed to (1) step into the true role of being in charge of his boys, (2) heal the sorely lacking sense of connection with each of his sons and between the two brothers, and (3) deal with the underlying elements contributing to the younger one's hurricane of rage and the older child's need to completely detach and numb himself with video games.

There are times when a child's refusal to cooperate is an indication of unspoken tension in the household, and his resistance is his attempt to exert even a little power within the context of feeling powerless. This may relate to constant bickering between parents, illness in a family member, or a difficult move. In this case, I urge parents to get suppressed problems and hurts out in the open where they can be properly addressed, and/or to seek the help of a trusted professional to help get the family back on track.

Evelyn and her eleven-year-old twin boys
Evelyn, a single mother, came to my workshop to get help with her eleven-year-old twin boys. "They won't do a thing I ask, whether it's turning down the TV while I'm on the phone, clearing the table after dinner, or taking their shower. It's impossible to get them to do anything I want unless they already want to do it! I'm at a loss. I've tried bribes, threats, behavior charts . . . the whole shebang. Nothing works, or at least nothing works for more than a couple of days. Then it's back to their old, defiant behavior!"

As the workshop progressed, I noticed Evelyn nodding her head a lot in agreement during the section on attachment and the need for parents to be the captains of the ship. She made a number of remarks suggesting that her attachment with the boys had become fractured; I acknowledged how especially challenging it can be to have twins, where issues of jealousy and comparison are ongoing.

"I can see so many ways where my connection to each of the boys has become weak. Matthew often complains that I take his brother's side [Belonging/Loyalty], and he's probably right. His motto is "It's not fair!" I think, too, that my frustration with his ongoing anger makes it pretty rare that I let him know that I really love him as he is [Significance; Love].

"As for Eddie, I put so much energy into managing Matthew's school problems and homework hassles that I don't spend nearly as much time with him [Proximity]. And I think I shut both boys down when they start telling me their problems [Being Known] by offering advice or criticism right away. (Act II) I imagine I'm not encouraging them to "tell me more" nearly as much as I'm talking them out of their feelings. They're probably holding a lot of hurt and anger inside. As I hear what you're saying about kids resisting direction when they don't have a sweet, solid connection with the person making the requests, it makes total sense to me that my boys don't do what I ask."

When I introduced the idea of being the captain of the ship, Evelyn got teary and told the rest of us that she felt she had long ago abandoned the hope of being truly in charge. "My boys really run the show. I try to assume authority by threatening and bribing, but looking at it from this new perspective, I can see now that they're actually the ones in charge."

Evelyn learned a number of ways to revive the connection with her boys and to restore her role as the one who is calmly and confidently in charge. In addition, I introduced her to the idea of turning a request into a *yes*, after first establishing a moment of connection.

Connecting, then directing

You tend to get a different response from a child when you holler from the other end of the house versus after making even a brief moment of friendly contact. If you sit beside him for a minute, showing interest in the model he's building or the program he's watching *before* you ask him to come to dinner, you'll get a more favorable response. *Connect, then direct.* Assuming that you're the calm, confident captain of the ship and that your attachment with the child is strong, taking a moment to connect *before* making a request can make an enormous difference in your child's willingness to cooperate.

Eye contact

Another add-on to this is to say, "Eyes on me," before making a request. This ensures the child is disengaged from whatever she was focused on and is at least semi-present for what you're about to say. Then, nod your head as you say, "It's time to head upstairs for your bath." As you nod, you're sending her a subtle suggestion to cooperate.

Requesting into the yes

With kids who are especially oppositional (and with almost all teens), it works much better to make a request if they've already said yes. In other words, you want a child or teen to already be nodding (literally or figuratively) to ensure a greater chance that he'll feel naturally inclined to do what you asked. I generally ask parents to try to get the child to nod or say "yes" three times prior to telling him to do something. This helps the child feel connected and heard, and also predisposes him to do what you ask. Here's a scenario that depicts connecting, then directing, and requesting into the yes:

> **Mom**: "It looks like you're having a lot of fun playing that video game."
> **Joseph**: "Sure am."
> **Mom**: "Is that guy in the yellow and purple one of the good guys, or is he somebody you're trying to avoid?"
> **Joseph**: "He's a hugely good guy—he's the guy who has the power gems that you have to get if you're going to pass through the Wicked Mountains!"
> **Mom**: "Oh! Is it hard to get to him?"
> **Joseph**: "Really hard. I've only done it once."
> **Mom**: "Wow. I guess it felt pretty good when you got to him, then."

Joseph: "Yeah, it was great!"

Mom: "It looks like it's a good challenge for you—not too easy, and not too hard."

Joseph: "Yep—that's right!"

Mom: "Thanks for showing me that, sweetie. Come along to dinner—and don't forget to wash up."

Joseph: "I'll be there in ten more minutes. I just have to finish this game."

Mom: "I know it's hard to stop, honey. But I'm afraid everybody's hungry, so we have to head on downstairs now."

Joseph: "Rats. Oh well. What are we having?"

Naturally, there are times when it's not this easy to get a child to come to dinner, but in this dialogue you get a feel for how things generally go when the parent-child relationship is in reasonably good shape and the parent connects with the child before directing him or her.

When parents routinely have problems getting their children to be agreeable despite using these approaches to make their requests, I encourage them to consider the *undercurrent* of the situation. This might include strengthening attachment by working through the Six Stages or by helping their children with chronic frustration, depression, or other issues that manifest in their refusal to do anything we ask, regardless of how friendly our approach.

Catch them being helpful

One of the easiest ways to encourage a child to be more cooperative is to help them feel good when they do. Try making a point of making three positive comments a day about something your child did. *This is not the same as praising them.* As odd as it might sound, I'm not a big fan of praise that sounds like, "You're such a good boy!" This positions the parent to be the judge of what is and isn't good, and can create an unhealthy addiction to parental approval, sabotaging the ultimate goal of a child doing the right thing because it feels good *internally*.

But if a child ends up coming to dinner the first time you

call, you can let them know how it felt *to you*: "I love seeing you at the table right after I called, sweetie! Thanks!" If they come downstairs quietly instead of stomping on each step as they often do, you might say, "Thanks for remembering to be extra quiet while the baby's sleeping." By showing your authentic appreciation for any evidence of thoughtfulness or cooperation, you create a natural desire for more. This is a basic, healthy way of helping a child learn to seek positive attention and connection, and discourages the acting out that many children use to get *any* parental attention.

Power struggles
In my workshops, I explain that many kids dig in their heels reflexively when we parents start engaging in power struggles about what they should and shouldn't do. As I mentioned earlier, it's instinctual to push back when force is used against us. When a child refuses to do what we ask and we respond by threatening, her impulse to resist is reinforced. Even if the threat compels her to do what we want, it comes at a price: resentment towards us.

I see a child's behavior as an *announcement*. When there's a problem, I ask, "What would she have to be feeling to behave this way?" It helps me to come *alongside* her rather than *at* her, which as we now know, provokes defensiveness, resistance, and withdrawal.

More often than not, when we make a request of our kids, we bring the aroma of our agenda spiced with a bit of anxiety about how they'll respond. Because of that, we rush to get to the Bottom Line, stumbling over ourselves as though getting our kids to agree to do their homework is the touchdown line and the only thing that matters is getting them there. They sense we're now in Power Struggle territory and often respond by digging in their heels, turning on what I call *Mom TV* to see what kind of drama we're going to create. Many kids get the most attention from their parents when they're in a power struggle with them. Why would a child want to cooperate when he gets 100 percent of Mom or Dad's attention only when he's stubborn and noncompliant?

> I see a child's behavior as an *announcement*. When there's a problem, I ask, "What would she have to be feeling to behave this way?"

One of the most popular approaches parents use is sending the errant child to her room for a timeout when she doesn't do what she's asked. The reason timeouts "work" is that they threaten the child's primal need for closeness (Proximity)—the entry point of attachment. This violation of connectedness damages the parent-child relationship, and the child pays for it with anxiety, clinginess, and other maladaptive behaviors.

While there are times when *we* need to leave the room because we can tell that we're getting increasingly worked up, it is not in the parent's or the child's best interest to resort to sending a child away when he is disobedient. One of Carl Jung's most important contributions to the field of psychology was to emphasize the importance of accepting the dark or shadow side that each of us invariably has and of learning to work *with* it rather than pretend it doesn't exist. The angry parent who ignores, shuns, or isolates the problematic child is effectively jumping ship, leaving the child without a captain and with the message that the child's shadow side is unacceptable. Timeouts may work well as a short-term solution, but the price a parent pays for using them, as their only method of managing children is unnecessarily high.

If, instead, we acknowledge that a child doesn't want to empty the dishwasher/do her homework/walk the dog, and we do so *without* losing our cool, we hold the position of being the captain of the ship and we let her see that these difficult interactions aren't battles with winners and losers. (By the way, I am *not* a fan of using war terminology such as "pick your battles" in the context of raising children.)

By managing our own reactions so we aren't depending on the child's behavior to make us feel we're in charge, we position ourselves to prevent the interaction from deteriorating if she doesn't cooperate. By giving her a chance to be heard and to feel understood—"I probably wouldn't want to walk the dog, either, if I were having fun playing a video game"—we sidestep the power struggle. It's sort of the Tai Chi approach. Without giving a youngster something to push against, there simply *is* no power struggle.

There is one other source of authority that parents often underestimate: **Silence**. When we *inhabit* the role of the one in charge, feeling it to the core, and simply give a child "The Look," we are "heard" most profoundly. Instead of using lots of words—which children invariably tune out—I frequently counsel parents to simply send a powerful look in their child's direction that captures the message "Did you *really* just say that?" This is one of the greatest tools in a parent's repertoire, and it is too often traded in for the far less effective use of long lectures.

Distraction

In my workshops, we call "Aunt Mary" a lot. Who is Aunt Mary, you ask? She's the fictitious auntie that we suddenly remember we absolutely must call *this very instant* when a child has gotten impossibly fixated on a demand and we need a gentle way to distract him. This obviously works better with younger children, but it can work very well with others.

> **Child**: *[after asking seven times why you can't go to the pet store and play with the puppies]* "Why, Mommy? Why can't we? It'll only take a minute! Why can't we? Why? We have to go *right now!*"
>
> **Mom**: "Oh my gosh! I forgot to call Aunt Mary!" And you promptly—but politely—excuse yourself to go in the other room to make that important call.

It also works if you suddenly have to go to the bathroom, find someone's phone number, or see if the toilet is running. Sometimes the kindest way to deal with a child who's stuck is simply to shift gears abruptly. Aunt Mary sometimes gets a *lot* of pretend phone calls!

Speak as though you're in charge, and use a big, fat period!

When you ask your child to do something, *speak as though you are in charge*. Kids have a tendency to tune us out when we go on and on about *why* they should do something, especially when we toss in lots of details. If you're asking a child to do something, deliver it as a statement rather than as a question. Instead of "Sweetie, it's time to clean up and take your bath, *okay?*" just say, "Sweetheart, time to clean up!" Make the request and put a BIG, FAT PERIOD at the end of the sentence. Walk away with the assumption that she's going to do what you ask. Don't hover and watch her vigilantly for signs that she's complying; it diminishes your authority. If you want your child to recognize that you're in charge, speak and act as though you are, with confidence.

> Make your request and then put a BIG, FAT PERIOD at
>
> the end of the sentence.

"I need you to . . ."
Similarly, be careful about couching a request in polite terms by saying, "Honey, I need you to brush your teeth/do your homework/organize your backpack. . . ." If you're in charge regardless of what your children do or don't do, then you certainly don't *need* them to brush their teeth! Instead, "It's time to brush your teeth, sweetie" is fine. Telling your kids you *need* them to do something undermines your authority.

If I need some help moving a piece of furniture or getting our dog into the bath, I certainly might say to my son, "Ari, I need you to help me get the dog into the bathtub." If I want him to clean up the mess he made with his buddies, I simply say, "Time to clean up that mess, guys!" For some, this may be splitting hairs or an issue of semantics; but for parents who want to understand how the language they use may be affecting their children's lack of cooperation, this shift could be helpful. Giving children the power to fulfill your need—or not—can prompt them to turn on *Mom TV* to see what you'll do if they don't comply.

"Yes, after . . ."
Another useful approach, especially with kids whose

oppositional brains are more easily awakened, is to avoid using the word "No" whenever possible and instead say, "Yes, after . . ." (This comes from Jane Fendelman[1], author of *Raising Humane Beings.*)

> **Child**: "Can I have another granola bar?"
> **Parent**: "Sure, after dinner!"
> **Child**: "Can James spend the night?"
> **Parent**: "Sounds like a plan! Next weekend should be great!"

This may not prevent a child from asking again anyway, but it softens the blow and helps keep his "Inner Lawyer" from waking up—you know, the one who excels in combating any and all explanations and information you might provide in response to that ubiquitous question "Why can't I?"

"It's just the right thing to do . . ."

Now and then I want my son to do something that he has absolutely no interest in doing. He's eighteen, and I like him to assert himself; I usually try to avoid power struggles with him when he protests so we can sort things out without a lot of drama. But sometimes we hit a stalemate.

Recently I told Ari we had been invited to drop by a very distant relative's house for a little going-away party. We had rarely socialized with this family, and my son felt it wasn't necessary. ("Lame" would more accurately describe his feelings about going.) I knew that their son—a few years younger than mine—had been through some rough times recently and that it might mean something to the family if we stopped by.

I said to Ari, "I'm not going to make you go. I don't want you to resent me for it or have a sulky attitude, and I have no interest in laying a guilt trip on you about why we should go. But here's the thing: It's the right thing to do."

I let him sit with it for a while, not forcing the issue, but I stood in my truth about the importance of wishing this family well before they moved away. When it came time to go to the party, I asked Ari if he would please come, and he got in the car without a fuss. When we appeal to our kids to be the best version of themselves—without lecturing or scolding—we give them more space to be who they want to be in their heart of hearts.

Back to Evelyn and her twin boys

About a week or so after the workshop she attended, Evelyn came to see me and offered the following update:

"I was skeptical at first about your idea that behavior problems often indicate problems in the parent-child relationship, but the more you talked about it, the more sense it made, so I promised myself I'd try your approach. I have to tell you that by just implementing a few things, my boys' behavior has gotten a *lot* better already. I've made a point of carving out a few minutes of time to listen to music with Eddie, and I'm stopping myself from forcing him to hear my advice when he starts to get mad. It's not like things are perfect, not by a long shot. But I can't deny the difference." Evelyn paused, trying to find the right words. "He seems softer ... more open to me, and he's not putting up such a battle when I ask him to help out."

Evelyn went on to tell me how things were going with her other son. "I think the thing that's really working with Matthew is coming *alongside* him instead of coming at him forcefully. I'm trying to avoid giving him anything to push against. I can see how my bossy approach—with things escalating if he resisted—made things deteriorate rapidly. The other thing that is making a huge difference with my boys is when I *Request into the Yes*. It's amazing how quickly things turned around in our house when I gave up on trying to control my kids' behavior and instead began focusing on *my* approach and working more from the standpoint of making a connection with them."

Getting kids to cooperate can be challenging, but let's face it: Most of us don't exactly trip over ourselves in our excitement to do our taxes or fold the laundry. Modeling your own willingness to deal with life's unpleasant tasks, coupled with working within a strong connection, should make things go more smoothly for everyone.

Questions and Suggestions

Question: *When I was a kid, if my parents said, "Take your shower" or "Do your homework," I just did it. Why is it that kids these days—including my own—think they don't have to do what we say simply "Because we say so!"?*

Suggestion: Many of us grew up in households where our parents' word was law, and there was no discussion, negotiation, or defying them. The problem with this style of parenting is that children who aren't allowed to have their voices heard feel powerless and often experience underlying resentment, frustration, or aggression.

As a result, many adults who had authoritarian parents decided to raise their own children differently. Where their parents might have refused to discuss what was being served for dinner, they now end up making little Susie a brand-new meal to "respect her preferences." Where your parent may have left no room for discussion around whether you could get your ears pierced, you may compensate for how angry you felt about that by letting your own daughter make these choices for herself, abdicating your role and authority. In my way of thinking, this is simply a matter of the pendulum swinging from one side to the other. I'm not promoting either extreme.

As easy as it is to say that your parents' approach worked, it came at a price. Children deeply need to feel that their views matter and that their parents are capable of listening to them with the respect they deserve. When you inhabit the role of being the captain of the ship in your child's life, you give her the opportunity to feel heard without feeling obligated to negotiate each request. As you get more comfortable using some of the strategies introduced in this book, you're going to see things getting easier. Sure, your kids may want you to explain why you don't want them to go to their friend's house after school or why they have to take a shower now and not after their TV show is over; but, as you've learned, you don't always have to engage in discussions and negotiations.

The more you remain lovingly connected and calmly in charge—*authentically* in charge, not just louder or able to take away things that they care about—the more you'll find your kids doing what you ask without making each request into an event. It may seem easier to simply overpower your children as your parents did you, but in the long run you can be in charge *and* be the kind of parent your kids want to emulate when they have children of their own.

***

Question: *Boy, am I good at this "Two Lawyers" thing. It's hard to imagine the kind of resolve it would take to not get pulled into negotiations with my kids. Can you say more about how to avoid getting into the back-and-forth dialogs with my son, who is clearly destined to become a lawyer one day?*

Suggestion: Believe me, I know how challenging it can be to resist the temptation to argue my case when my son and I have serious differences in opinion. There are plenty of times I slip into Lawyer mode before I realize what's happened. I'm not saying it's easy. For those of us who grew up in households where Being Right felt like winning, we learned how to convincingly line up facts in our favor and dismiss the other person's point of view so we could prevail. The reality, however, is that when we engage in power struggles and heated arguments with our kids, no one "wins." The kids don't feel their opinions are being heard or respected, and the parents no longer come across as calmly in charge.

Please don't misunderstand me. There is absolutely nothing wrong with discussing situations with your kids when you disagree. Far be it from me to promote a "my way or the highway" approach to parenting. I think it's tremendously important that we engage in back-and-forth dialogue with our kids; it's one of the best ways for them to learn to use their voice and explore their beliefs and convictions. But there's a time and a place for good old-fashioned debate.

When you, as the parent, know that it's not in your child's best interests to stay up late or have a third helping of chocolate cake before bed, it's much kinder to help her feel heard and perhaps walk her to the Wall of Futility than to fuel her frustration by arguing. There's no positive outcome to "The Two

Lawyers." In the end, somebody—whoever is more stubborn, willful, or threatening—will get her way, and the other will feel resentful or disempowered.

Since most changes happen incrementally, give yourself room to let these ideas simmer and take root. If you find yourself in Lawyer mode with your child, let it play out and pat yourself on the back for even *noticing* that you slipped into that role. This is how things shift: First we make mistakes unconsciously, without any awareness; then there are those "Whoops!" moments when we notice we've behaved in ways we had resolved to change and we can celebrate the fact that we're becoming more aware; finally, we start catching ourselves *about* to slip into Lawyer mode and instead we come *alongside* our child, not at her. By setting the intention to change, those times start happening more and more frequently.

Learn and implement these ideas in your own time. Make mistakes, notice that you've made them, and do your best next time. Acknowledge the times when you've stayed out of the fray and have maintained your position as the captain of the ship. The more you do this, the more easily it will happen naturally.

***

Question: *I like the idea of getting my kids nodding and feeling connected to me before I ask them to do something. But sometimes I just want them to get in the car for school or soccer practice, and I can't imagine having to jump through all these hoops every time. Isn't this awfully time consuming?*

Suggestion: It seems time consuming at first, but I guarantee you, the parents who have used this approach tell me again and again that it greatly reduces the time and energy it takes to get kids to do what they ask. This doesn't mean that each and every time you want your children to come to dinner you have to find each one individually, sit beside them to connect, and serenely ask them to join you at the table. If you make sure the connection you have with your kids is generally strong and healthy and if you use these ideas as much as possible, I think you'll find that ultimately it saves lots of time by avoiding prolonged arguments and negotiations, making life with your kids more enjoyable.

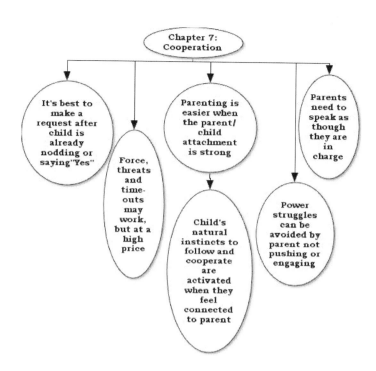

Chapter Eight
Celebrate the Child You've Got

"Welcome to Agape. We recognize you. We know who you truly are. You are a unique way in which love, intelligence, and divine beauty are happening on this planet. We celebrate you. We appreciate you. And we thank God for you."

(What guests at Agape International Spiritual Center hear when they attend for the first time. For many, hearing these words delivered with such loving kindness prompts a spontaneous flow of tears.)

Not long ago, I was visiting friends at their twenty-acre home on the big island of Hawaii. Gwen and Micah have five dogs: Blue, Bree, Lila, Ole, and Zorro. Each of these animals has a well-defined personality and temperament. Blue's the sniffer—he makes sense of his world by smelling everything he comes in contact with. Ole's the licker—he needs to taste you to see if you're going to be his friend! Bree's the watchdog, sounding the alarm and getting the other dogs going when someone arrives or leaves. Lila is very protective, always scolding Bree, Blue, and Ole (her pups) and bossing them around. And Zorro—being a rescued dog—is still very cautious. You can't make any moves in his direction; you have to wait patiently for him to come to you. But he roams the property with a smile from ear to ear, spreading joy wherever he goes.

We accept the different ways the dogs manifest their individual natures, and find them endlessly entertaining. Instead of trying to mold them to be different from what they are, we revel in their distinctive personalities. Gwen knows that she needs to approach Zorro slowly. Micah knows he needs to give Blue time to smell him all over every morning. The dogs are given the freedom to be who they are.

What if we approached our children this way? What if we marveled at their personalities and interests instead of trying to force them to be something other than the perfect expression of life that they are?

Ask parents what they want for their children, and success in some form is always the answer. Whatever your definition, one of the core elements for launching children towards a successful life begins with them feeling accepted and cherished for who they are, as is, right now, regardless of their grades or their behavior. The mad dash to have more, be more, and do more reflects the deep insecurity I see in so many of my adult clients who believe that who they are just isn't enough. Clearly, who they were as children was not acceptable, and they headed towards adulthood on an endless quest for approval and appreciation.

Parents don't realize how potent their acceptance—or the lack thereof—is to their children. We discount the greatest gift we can give our kids, which is simply to revel and rejoice in who they are, with their special gifts and talents as well as their weaknesses and challenges.

Frequently, I'll have an experience like one I recently had with Janice, a fifty-seven-year-old client. She tearfully related a story about her eighty-four year old parent's disapproval about something she had done a few days before, recounting how discouraged she was by her mother's lack of enthusiasm for her decision to make some changes in her work life. Even though my client is theoretically all grown-up, she still struggles with the disappointment of not getting her mom's approval! Naturally, we worked therapeutically around Janice's need to step more fully into her choices, regardless of whether or not she has her mother's endorsement. But I couldn't help but be touched by how profoundly she still longed to be appreciated and seen for who she was by her mom.

Children who are joyful and authentic catch glimpses of their mother or father looking at them with wonder and love, not because they've just accomplished something or done what they were told, but simply because they exist. Happy children feel *liked* by their parents and know that who they are in their hearts and minds is pleasing. There's a sense of being known intimately, and that what is known about them is worthy of strengthening the bond they have with their caregiver.

Sometimes we need help coming around to accepting our children as they are. What follows is a process I went through with a father I'll call Dennis. After you read through this scenario, you'll have a chance to do some of your own reflection around any resistance or challenges you might experience towards certain characteristics of your children. I strongly encourage you to dive in and do the work so you can see your kids for the remarkable human beings they are!

Dennis and his artistic son

Dennis was the father of a very talented twelve-year-old boy. Michael was fascinated with Japanese animation; he participated in anime websites, watched and recorded the shows on TV, and filled the backside of every piece of paper (including the margins of his homework) with his drawings. When we met, Dennis was frustrated and confused by his son's poor grades and his refusal to study harder for tests. He felt his son was wasting his time on something irrelevant and that he should try out for some kind of sport, since his anime "obsession" meant he was always indoors and not physically active.

I asked Dennis to write out a list of things that upset or frustrated him about Michael. Here is his list:

- He doesn't care enough about his schoolwork.
- He's always drawing on things.
- He spends time watching stupid shows, like *Yu-Gi-Oh!*
- He should spend more time outside being physically active.
- He should do more boy stuff and be more athletic.

Next, I asked Dennis to tell me the feelings that came up for him as he read each item on this list. He mentioned words such as "frustrated," "worried," "embarrassed," and "helpless." Using the Four Questions (see Chapter 1), we embarked on a process to shine a revealing light on the thoughts and stories Dennis told himself about his son, so we could separate the actual truth from the unquestioned, knee-jerk thoughts that landed between his ears and triggered his upsetting judgments, feelings, and reactions. What follows is the exercise we went through around one of Dennis' upsetting thoughts: *Michael should spend more time outside being physically active.*

Susan: "One thing you've written is that Michael should

spend more time outside being physically active. Is it true, Dennis?"

Dennis: "Yes, it's true! The boy needs to exercise and get out in the fresh air!"

Susan: "Can you absolutely know that it's true that Michael should spend more time outside being physically active?"

Dennis: "Well, I guess I can't absolutely know that it's true, but I sure think he should! It's not good for a kid to be inside all day, watching shows or drawing."

Susan: "I understand. And how do you feel, or how do you react, when you believe the thought that Michael should spend more time outside being physically active?"

Dennis: "Well, I feel frustrated and irritated, and kind of ashamed of Michael, like he's a baby. And then I worry about him—I think he's not going to be tough enough to make it if he's inside drawing or chatting online with artists about this hobby of his instead of getting exercise and toughening up."

Susan: "When you're feeling those things, how are you around Michael, Dennis?"

Dennis: "I'm edgy and irritable and definitely not friendly towards him. I scold him for refusing to do what I've insisted is right for him—get outside for at least forty-five minutes a day. Pretty much every interaction we have, from the time I walk in the door and see Michael drawing or watching one of those anime shows, is negative."

Susan: "Dennis, who would you be without this thought, or this story, that Michael should spend more time outside being physically active? I'm not asking you to drop the desire for him to get outside and exercise, but I'm just asking you to consider this: Who would you be, or how might you be different, if you weren't gripped by this belief, which seems to make you edgy and irritable and unfriendly? If that upsetting thought were a pill, who would you be if you didn't swallow it?"

Dennis: "Well, I'd be much more relaxed. I'd just be happy to see my son, instead of thinking about how he's not doing what I think he should be doing. I guess I'd be more easy-going around him... and that might end up motivating him at least a little to do something outside with me once in a while! At least I wouldn't have this tension around him all the time."

The turnaround

Susan: "So, Dennis, let's look at the turnaround to this thought. Can you think of at least three reasons why it might be true—or even truer—that Michael *shouldn't* spend more time outside being physically active? I'm not asking you to shut the boy indoors from now on; I'm just asking you to stretch your thinking and consider how it might be that there's some value in things being just as they are."

Dennis: "Why he *shouldn't* spend more time outside being physically active? Wow. All right, I'll give it a go. Let's see. Well, one reason might be that he doesn't like it. He's a bit like his mother in that way; she isn't big on nature and all that—she loves painting and puttering around the house. And maybe another reason would be that he's trying really, really hard to get good at this anime drawing thing. I have to admit that his drawings are pretty exceptional; he's gotten a lot better in the last year or so, and a lot of his drawings are as good as the stuff on those shows he watches. Maybe a third reason he shouldn't spend more time outside being active would be... hmmm ... This is tough. Okay. How about this? A third reason would be that it's his way of rebelling against me. It's sort of the one area where he can stand up to me. After all, the kid pretty much has to do what he's told all day by teachers, and he doesn't even enjoy his classes, and then he comes home and has to help around the house. It might just be the only area in his life where he can stand up for himself and dig in his heels and say no to what somebody's trying to make him do. How's that?"

Susan: "I think that's a pretty insightful thing you just said, Dennis. It seems like you're able to see this from another vantage point by being less in the grip of your original story."

Dennis: "I think I've got a lot to think about. Looking at it this way, I can already see some things that are making sense to me about my boy."

Dennis realized he'd been projecting onto Michael some of the disappointment he'd been feeling about his *own* lack of working out the way he used to, and his upset about having dropped the weekly basketball pick-up game he used to love playing with his buddies. He ended up exploring with Michael some of the "benefits" (from the turnarounds) that he'd put on the right side of his paper. Michael was genuinely astonished when his dad asked him about his reluctance to spend time outside and then listened to what his son had to *say without offering advice or making demands of him.* (Act I) The conversation deepened and Michael opened up about how frustrating school was, and how burnt-out he felt having to spend all day doing things he had little interest in doing.

Dennis then sat and looked through Michael's drawings and began to feel a swelling pride in his son's talent. A few days later he helped Michael make a proper portfolio of some of his best drawings, and he framed his favorite, hanging it in the hall outside his bedroom. Michael asked his dad to go for a bike ride with him the next weekend, and the relationship continued to improve as Dennis did the work to help him see Michael—and cherish him—for exactly who he was.

Dennis worked with me for another month or two. He was finally willing to feel the grief he had about not having a boy who was more into sports the way he was, which then liberated him to see the wonderful son he *did* have. Michael began to blossom; he took a summer art class in anime, and the next year, while continuing his passion for that, his grades in school started to go up. Dennis gave his son a priceless gift: He *saw* him, in all his beauty and giftedness, thereby setting Michael on the road towards being and becoming the best version of himself possible.

When children are liberated from their parents' dissatisfaction with who they are and should be, they're freed up to rise to their true potential, with all the accompanying joy and satisfaction that comes from being exactly who they were meant to be.

Exercise—Moving towards accepting our child as is

Take out a sheet of paper and fold it in half. On the left side of the page, write down the behaviors, qualities, or characteristics that you find frustrating or difficult to accept in your child. Talk aloud—to the cat or to your favorite tree—about what emotions come up for you around these behaviors or qualities in your child. Be honest and present in the moment, and allow your real feelings the space they need to find expression. If this process is extremely emotional or brings up deep sadness or anger, you may find it valuable to work through some of your emotions with a trusted therapist.

Now, create a sentence for each of the "judgments" you had about your child. It often helps if you use the word "should" or "shouldn't" in your sentence. *Julie should be more outgoing*, or *Brian shouldn't be so disorganized*. Follow through this process with whichever qualities or behaviors you have on the left side of your paper. (Don't be surprised if you find that a quality you have trouble accepting in your child is a version of one that you have trouble accepting in yourself.)

The right side of the page—the turnarounds

On the right side of the page, list at least one turnaround—or possible benefit—for each of the characteristics or behaviors you listed on the left side of the page. Often the very quality that bugs you or is problematic for your child turns out to be her greatest learning opportunity (or yours) when seen in a different light. You may also discover that this annoying quality—such as being argumentative or stubborn—may be an essential quality that will serve her later in life. By accepting a tendency or quality you find challenging in your child—instead of arguing with it— you become open to seeing that it may be at least temporarily serving her. This puts you, as captain of the ship, in a position to directly recognize and meet your child's needs, instead of requiring her to take on maladaptive, annoying behaviors to accomplish that.

Dahlia and her exceptional sons

Not long ago I found myself at a party with an acquaintance. I knew little about Dahlia's personal life, other than the fact that she was married and had two sons. But I had always liked her; she seemed very grounded and happy in her life. So I was pleased when we were at a dinner together and I had the chance to get to know more about her.

> By coming *alongside* a quality you find challenging in your child—instead of *fighting* it—you become open to seeing that it may be serving your child.

Within moments, as is often the case, someone asked Dahlia about her kids. She started to glow and said she had two awesome sons. The older boy, a highly gifted fourteen-year-old, was a lifeguard that summer and pursuing a number of outside interests as well. Her younger son, the eleven-year-old, was the *sweetest* child. It wasn't until she elaborated that I discovered her eleven-year-old could only communicate through primitive sounds and sign language that only his family members could decode, and that he still wore diapers. What amazed me was that this was not the first thing Dahlia mentioned when she was asked about her kids, nor was it—to her—the most important. When I asked her what it was like having such a tremendously high-need child (with all the accompanying demands and restrictions) in addition to her other very gifted son, she just looked at me, smiled, and said, "You know, people often look at me with pity or awe, asking how I do it; but . . . it's just my life. It's just what I do. I love it!"

Clearly this was someone who had discovered how to celebrate each of her children and had let go of whatever resistance she might have had to the mismatch between what her family was *supposed* to look like and the reality of it. As a result, she was living a joyful, peaceful life. When you give your children the gifts of acceptance and, even greater, of celebrating them exactly as they are, you equip them to live joyous, fulfilled lives, while enjoying enjoy the journey of their childhood with a sense of adventure, ease and gratitude.

Questions and Suggestions

Question: *You say that it's vital for parents to accept their children as they are, but what about children whose behavior is nasty—meaning, in a sense they're not really* being *who they truly are?*

Suggestion: I understand from personal experience that we all have times when we become "possessed" by some altered version of ourselves that makes it difficult for even an adoring mother to have warm feelings. I also know, again from personal experience, that when I'm not being "myself," I desperately want to be.

Who better to help a child come back to his true self than a parent? But if we're allowing ourselves to be personally offended by a child's nasty behavior, it can be nearly impossible to guide him. When your child manifests particularly dark and unpleasant qualities of his personality, your first challenge as the captain of the ship is to step back and look at what *meaning* you're assigning to his behavior. Notice if you're turning his refusal to help you unload the dishwasher into an epic story, like "He *never* does what I ask! He doesn't appreciate *anything* I do for him! He's lazy and spoiled!"

Remember that you, too, sometimes fall prey to fatigue, dark clouds, or hunger-provoked crankiness. If you're chronically worn-out, eating poorly, or at the mercy of other life stressors, it's going to be harder to handle your kid's difficult behavior. Remember the saying "When Mom's happy, everybody's happy." Naturally, this applies equally to anyone caring for a child. Make sure you're not just running on fumes, and take care of yourself.

If you can maintain your position as captain, you'll be able to think in reverse to the series of events that might have contributed to your child's nasty behavior and thus diminish its impact on you.

Generally speaking, I find that the things in my own son's behavior that trigger me the most are the same things I find hard to face ruthlessly in myself. Using inquiry, you may find yourself able to see that the apple indeed doesn't fall far from the tree. This doesn't always mean that when a child is poorly behaved it's because she's mimicking Mom or Dad, but there's usually an element in a child's off-putting behavior that's painfully familiar. If you can come *alongside* your child by imagining the world through her current experience rather than pushing *against* her, you'll be headed towards a place where you can accept her as she is in this moment, even if she's manifesting her shadow side. This might include looking at ways that *you* sometimes act spoiled and unappreciative. And sometimes you'll need some time and space to find the adult version of yourself that's capable of sorting this out. That's all right, too. Just don't make it your child's job to make you feel okay.

***

Question: *I know I should accept my child, but honestly, I struggle with the fact that she is so dramatically different from me. I hate to say this about my own daughter, but she's terribly self-absorbed and only interested in things like fashion and makeup that don't mean anything to me and seem awfully superficial. How do I accept this?*

Suggestion: Again, it's usually the things we judge most harshly in others (including our children) that we have going on in some way within ourselves. So, my first piece of advice would be to invite you to find out how the criticisms you have about your daughter might apply in some way to yourself. Perhaps you're not involved in things as frivolous as fashion and makeup, but if you're upset by those interests in your daughter, there's a good chance there is *something* you do that others might consider frivolous. (This could include the fact that you readily judge others who are interested in makeup and fashion!)

Too often we become so distracted by characteristics in our children that are at odds with our own interests or preferences that we miss the many ways they *do* embody the things we value. I would ask you to make a list of your daughter's qualities and passions—perhaps enlisting the help of family friends and relatives—to broaden the picture you have of her. It's easy to take a snapshot of someone—including your own child—and see them only from one vantage point. My guess is that although her *primary* interests right at this moment might be fashion and makeup, there are other things about her that may be getting eclipsed by your focus on those particular things. Is she funny? Does she like to sing? Is she attentive to her grandma? Do little kids follow her around? There's a good chance that you're missing things about her that are worthy of paying more attention to, which in itself will help you be less uncomfortable with the ways in which the two of you differ.

As you read in Chapter 2, one of your daughter's most fundamental needs is to be lovingly attached to you. I empathize with you insofar as it can be easier to enjoy Proximity, Sameness, and Significance with a child who's more naturally like you. But if you drop the judgments you have about her, you'll become able to explore facets of your daughter that you might have ignored, allowing you to come to an authentic appreciation for who she is. Along with a strong attachment between the two of you will come the natural endearment that makes her less-desirable qualities become tolerable, while liberating you to find the treasures that may lie undiscovered in her nature.

***

Question: *I love my child to the moon and back. We're an older couple who tried for years to have him, and we will not be having more children. But Devon is developmentally delayed, and there are times when I feel very sad about his limitations, especially when I see other children his age doing things he can't do. How can I help from feeling guilty when I have these feelings?*

Suggestion: I understand. Please don't feel guilty about your disappointment; it's natural to want your child to be able to do and experience all of life with ease and enjoyment, and it's human for you to need to grieve about your son's limitations. More importantly, if you pretend you don't have feelings that are real for you, they'll just go underground where they'll fester and quietly drain you or turn into resentment. It would be far better to look the darker side of your emotions squarely in the eye and process them now rather than ignore them out of guilt or discomfort.

So, the first recommendation I would offer you is to spend some time just sitting with your sorrow. Give space to the feelings. Allow them room to simply be. I often tell my clients that each challenging event or loss in our lives becomes a room in our house. Rather than letting that room become musty by closing the doors and sealing the windows, in order to maintain good psychological health we need to open the room up and sit in it for a while.

When we let our sadness find expression, it begins to soften. As that happens, try using the Four Questions around a thought that is particularly painful. This might be, *"Devon will never be as happy as other people"* or *"Because he's developmentally delayed, our son won't have any friends who accept him just as he is."* Walk through the Four Questions and take special care with the Turnarounds.

By shining a bright light on the idea that *"Because of his developmental delays, Devon won't have friends who accept him just as he is,"* you'll look for three specific examples of how it might be as true *or truer* that *"Because of his developmental delays, Devon* will *have friends who accept him just as he is."* Just as a lawyer takes a premise and finds evidence to support it, look for proof that your son *will* have friends. Notice other children with developmental delays who have friends, either in your immediate world or via support groups or the Internet. Remind yourself of the many children *without* a label or diagnosis who are often friendless, either because they are naturally more solitary or they haven't figured out yet how to make and keep friends. Widen your circle to include other children who are developmentally delayed and are living happy lives.

This activity is not meant to simply get you to cheer up and think positive thoughts. It's more than an exercise in looking on the bright side. By diving straight into the stories that trigger your sadness and looking at how those beliefs may genuinely be untrue, you can come out the other side with a real sense of the blessings surrounding your son.

This doesn't mean you won't feel sad from time to time about his limitations. Nor am I suggesting that if you get stuck in your sorrow you shouldn't avail yourself of supportive psychological help with a trusted counselor. Doing so might be very helpful. But by fully moving *into* your feelings rather than hiding from them, you'll be better equipped to loosen their grip on you so that you can step into the fullness of the joy of parenting the child you have been blessed with.

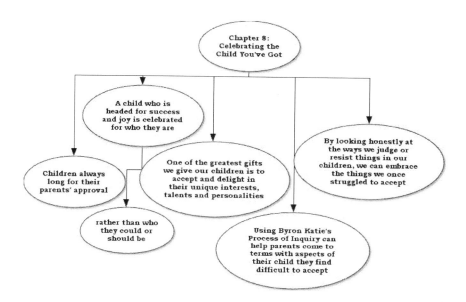

Chapter 8: Celebrating the Child You've Got

A child who is headed for success and joy is celebrated for who they are

Children always long for their parents' approval

rather than who they could or should be

One of the greatest gifts we give our children is to accept and delight in their unique interests, talents and personalities

Using Byron Katie's Process of Inquiry can help parents come to terms with aspects of their child they find difficult to accept

By looking honestly at the ways we judge or resist things in our children, we can embrace the things we once struggled to accept

Chapter Nine
Every Kid's a Genius

"The word genius was whispered into my ear, the first thing I ever heard, while I was still mewling in my crib. So it never occurred to me that I wasn't until middle age."
Orson Welles

When most of us think of a genius, we picture somebody who wears pocket protectors, gets straight A's in school, and is wildly successful in some entrepreneurial endeavor that we wish we'd thought of ourselves if only we were—a genius! Kids who get into Harvard are geniuses. Einstein was a genius . . . but *my* kid? The one outside riding his bike across the neighbor's lawn who can't remember his multiplication tables? I don't think so.

The truth is, we need to redefine the word. Imagine what our lives would be like if intelligence came in just one color and our world was a drab, monochromatic landscape with everything the same hue. Picture what life would be like with everyone competent at reading and writing, cleverly putting their thoughts into words or solving complex mathematical problems, but without musicians, athletes, dancers, or painters. Imagine a world void of animal lovers, philosophers, or gentle caretakers who may have failed at math but whose presence soothes and nourishes you to your core.

Thomas Armstrong, the author of *7 Kinds of Smart*, defines the word "genius" as meaning "to give birth" (from "genesis") or "to be zestful or joyous" (from "genial"). He goes on to say that the real meaning of genius is to "give birth to the joy" that is within each child, stating that the ancient Romans used "genius" to refer to a guardian spirit that protected people throughout their lives. The question isn't whether or not our child is a genius; it's simply *what type* of genius they are.

How we learn
Psychologist Howard Gardner[1] has come up with eight forms of intelligence that encompass the various forms of human potential.

These are Logic/Mathematic, Verbal/Linguistic, Visual/Spatial, Body/Kinesthetic, Musical, Interpersonal, In*tra*personal, and Naturalist. Every human being has the potential for greatness in at least one of these areas, and often in many. We each come equipped with the ability to intuitively understand how to do something. This might mean knowing how to create beautiful music, design a garden, or write poetry. In fact, most people gifted in their field cannot adequately tell you *why* they're good at what they do; it just comes naturally.

> Gardner's eight classifications of intelligence are Logic/Mathematic, Verbal/Linguistic, Visual/Spatial, Body/Kinesthetic, Musical, Interpersonal, In*tra*personal, and Naturalist.

Each and every child is born with his or her own flavor of brilliance, arriving on Planet Earth fueled by curiosity, imagination, and wonder. As children grow, their natural gifts are meant to find expression, whether related to their love of music, language, or any number of other realms of delight. If we truly understood how essential each type of intelligence is to our collective enjoyment of life—not to mention our survival—we would be excited to discover our children's innate gifts and would do all we could to nurture them, whatever they were.

But we live in a society where the dollar rules and, generally speaking, the highest salaries are paid to those most proficient in mathematic and language skills. Because of this, schools reward those children who are naturally skilled in logic/mathematic and verbal/linguistic intelligence. We tend to minimize the giftedness of children with other forms of intelligence, underestimating the value of their contribution, and encouraging them to focus on developing mastery in areas where they're weakest.

Teachers, constrained by having to "teach to the test," are required to devote the vast majority of their time to developing their students' reading, writing, and math abilities, which means that children who are otherwise gifted will find school boring, tiring, and difficult. And because those children who are naturally gifted in reading and math get good grades and gold stars—often with relatively little effort—they are perceived as brighter than their musical or interpersonally intelligent counterparts.

Kids without natural abilities in logic/mathematics or verbal/linguistics often see themselves as stupid. They are frequently told that they could do better if they simply tried harder, applied themselves, weren't so lazy, or paid closer attention. These are kids who may be absolutely brilliant at getting to know people, building a go-kart, or concocting an award-winning dessert, but because they are consistently told they must improve their schoolwork, they may never taste the thrill that comes from manifesting their special gifts.

We know that one of the common denominators reported by people with a high degree of personal satisfaction in their daily lives is that they are engaged in work or activities that are in synch with their passions. As parents, when we help our kids identify and nurture their unique interests and talents as they grow up, we contribute greatly to the possibility that, as adults, they will fall into step with work that enriches, challenges, and excites them—all of which predispose them to awakenening to each morning with a sense of aliveness that infuses their day with meaning and joy.

The challenge for parents is this: Most children spend close to sixteen thousand hours of their formative years in an environment that may not nurture their interests. *Sixteen thousand hours* of our children's lives are a *lot* of hours. If you happen to have a youngster who does well in school, then much of his day he's feeling successful, or at least competent. But for those kids whose natural talents fall outside the spectrum of what is generally taught in school, every day can be painful and exhausting.

Your new job is going to be doing taxes every day!

Imagine this: I get to decide what your profession is going to be. And I've decided that I want your job to be doing taxes. You're going to be doing taxes five days a week, six to seven hours a day. Any tax returns you don't finish during the day will need to be finished in the evening. In addition, I'm going to have you do some *practice* tax work most evenings to help you sharpen your skills. You're going to have this job nine and a half months a year for twelve years. For the most part, you are not to talk with others while doing taxes. Also, your work needs to be tidy, clean, and accurate. In addition, if you dawdle in the morning instead of moving efficiently so you can get out of the house and be on time for your tax job, I'm going to threaten, punish, or shame you. If you complain about going to your tax job, I will lecture you. If you balk at doing the extra tax work you're given to do in the evenings, I will scold you.

Imagine how it feels to face this kind of life, day in and day out, with no light at the end of the tunnel until you're finally on the home stretch, which takes place some time in year eleven (of the twelve years). If doing taxes is difficult for you—or simply unpleasant—consider the potential for depression, fatigue, and powerlessness you would feel at having been given this job assignment. Imagine the longing you would feel to be out riding your horse, if that was your passion, or composing music, if that was your love. Likewise, consider the impact on a child whose natural gifts are not nurtured or rewarded in a typical classroom.

When I ask most children what they like about school, the answer I'm almost always given is "recess." Even kids who do well in school don't usually leap out of bed in the morning to arrive on time. Yet those same kids will be up bright and early on weekends or vacations because they're eager to do what children do best: enjoying life, having fun, and learning about whatever fascinates them.

Babies are irrepressible learners. They insist on exploring, tasting, and devouring new experiences; this urge is driven by their innate passion for learning. A young child would rather learn than eat. In fact, if you ask most people when their passion for learning started to diminish, the answer you'll hear most frequently will be "around the age of five or six." Coincidentally, this is when we start school.

You might think I'm proposing a mass exodus from traditional classrooms in favor of home schooling. On the contrary, I think many children thrive in school. More and more innovations are being brought into classrooms that make learning more enjoyable. And for kids who are social, schools offer the opportunity not only to play with friends but also to stay engaged by learning with them.

You may also get the feeling that I believe it's not important that all children learn to read, write, and do mathematics. Again, this is untrue. To deprive a child of the ability to read and write is to disadvantage them for life. I simply believe that children need to be supported *in their best learning style* to master academics rather than be subjected to a one-size-fits-all teaching approach that simply doesn't work for everybody.

I am a wholehearted advocate for helping teachers learn methods that will encourage *all* the children in their classrooms to learn and succeed according to the strengths of their natural intelligence. But as with everything else, it is ultimately the parent's responsibility to call forth and nurture their child's innate talents and passions.

One of the most potent ways to inspire a child to be passionate about learning is *to be* passionate about learning. The way you live in front of your kids can either dampen or spark their thirst for exploring their interests and expressing their unique brand of genius. Regardless of your day job, are you making time to paint, learn French, or garden? Do you stay within your comfort zone, or are you stretching yourself beyond the unfamiliar to advance your skills? Do your kids see you being playful as you learn, reveling in the sheer pleasure of expanding your knowledge? Are they able to watch you develop your creativity, whether it's learning salsa dancing, taking up short-story writing, or drumming? If so, your children are getting the message that learning is a lifelong activity that enhances one's enjoyment of life.

The way you live in front of your kids can either dampen or spark their thirst for exploring their interests and expressing their unique brand of genius.

When parents turn their kids over to the TV or video game box, they are, to be blunt, dumbing them down. "But my kids need to veg out and recover from their day," many parents tell me, "and so do I. It would be hypocritical of me to tell them to turn off the TV when I'm in the next room watching it myself so I can relax after a long day of work." I'll say more about this later, but for now, consider this: Human beings grow and thrive on creativity, stimulation, and challenge.

Children who are gifted in areas that get little attention in school *need to shine regularly* in their own particular ways. It's up to parents to first identify their children's interests and then provide opportunities to develop those skills outside of the school day. These might include art classes, music lessons, or learning to juggle from the guy who does street theater on the weekends down at the local boardwalk. It's vital that parents advocate on behalf of their children's natural interests and give them the chance to develop their unique abilities.

I recently read a touching story written by a young adult who described the various labels he was given throughout his schooling. When he was a boy, Legos, puzzles, and gadgets fascinated him, and his loving mother encouraged his excitement and passion. But in the school setting where there were few hands-on activities, he withdrew and shut down mentally and emotionally; teachers thought he was mildly retarded. He was diagnosed as developmentally delayed and eventually placed in special classes, where he shut down even more. As he grew into adolescence, he became frustrated, angry, and rebellious; he was diagnosed with obsessive-compulsive disorder, ADHD, and oppositional defiant disorder. He said, "Throughout my years at school there was not one person who took the time to connect with my passion. No one cared or understood what made me tick. They just wanted me to fit into some box."

Finally, as a young adult, while interviewing for a custodial position, the interviewer drew him out, expressing a genuine interest in finding out what he liked to do in his spare time. When he shyly told her about his passion for building and fixing, she told him their company desperately needed someone to repair things in the service department. For the first time he began to build true self-confidence and know the satisfaction that comes from expressing one's natural born gifts.

When genius is wrapped in a package labeled ADD

Over the years, many parents have brought children into my office labeled as having ADD by a teacher, pediatrician, mother-in-law, or neighbor. My general response used to be to subtly roll my eyes and tell the parent that I didn't think there was such a thing as Attention Deficit Disorder. It was my opinion that what appeared to be ADD was really a learning-style incompatibility between the child and the teacher. In other words, if a youngster was a right-brained, auditory learner and the teacher was more of a left-brained, visual teacher, the child would inevitably get bored and begin daydreaming, chatting with kids sitting near him, or fidgeting to distraction, just as you or I would do if we were sitting in on a lecture that was being delivered in a language we didn't speak.

I still believe that some children have a learning-style incompatibility and not ADD. Many kids are kinesthetic, hands-on learners; and when they're taught in a more project-based way or with a variety of avenues for taking in information, they do very well and their "ADD-ish" behavior fades away entirely. I also believe—staunchly—that the ADD label is grossly inaccurate in describing children or adults who have the constellation of symptoms that pegs them with this diagnosis. Most people—even those who have tremendous difficulties paying attention for a sustained period of time—can concentrate when they're *interested*. (More on that soon.)

In addition, nearly everyone I know (and certainly almost everyone I *like*) falls somewhere on the ADD spectrum when it comes to symptoms of impulsivity, distractibility and attraction to whatever's new, bright, and shiny. But having said all that, I do believe there are some children who have *something* that makes it really hard for them to focus for any length of time, to sit still, or to manage their impulses, and I believe that *some* of those children struggle because of how their brains are functioning.

Once I accepted this possibility, I was able to find ways

to explain the challenges of staying focused and managing impulsivity that removed the blame, shame, and judgment from the picture. This opened the possibilities for ADD-ish children—and their parents—to work *together* to develop strategies to make it easier for them to function successfully in a world that isn't always fascinating, hands-on, and engaging.

The first valuable bit of information comes from Dr. Daniel Amen, the innovative psychiatrist who improved our understanding of ADD (and many other psychiatric challenges) by his use of Spect scans of the brain. While I understand that there are some who find the scans controversial, Dr. Amen has paved the way for thousands of people to understand the brain by allowing them to *see* it.

The area behind your forehead is known as the prefrontal cortex, or the PFC, which is also referred to as the executive center of the brain because it's especially important in functions such as planning, organizing, managing impulses, sustaining attention, and so on. Someone who is highly impulsive, easily distracted, very disorganized, "spacey," and forgetful may produce a Spect scan of their prefrontal cortex that shows an excess amount of *slow* brain wave activity—*if* these symptoms are neurologically based. This has absolutely nothing to do with intelligence. And when that same individual is engaged in an activity that is highly stimulating to him, his PFC will show normal, alert brain wave activity.

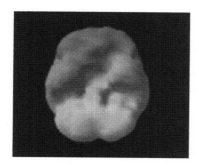
Normal Brain

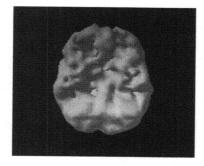
"ADDish" Brain

At this point, let me address the problem I have with the ADD label, which is why I keep calling it "ADD-ish." I believe people who produce excess slow activity in the PFC don't have a *deficit* of attention; instead, it's more a case of there being *inflexibility* in their attention. In other words, they aren't *in charge* of what they focus on. Instead, whatever *yanks* on their attention is what they pay attention to.

I also don't see ADD as a disorder, per se. It can certainly contribute to problems, both academically and psychologically (ADD is a major contributor to depression, for example, and is very often accompanied by anxiety as well). But there are many happy, highly functional people who are successful, not just *in spite* of their ADD but probably *because* of it (myself included). People with ADD are highly creative, spontaneous, energetic, interesting, sensitive, charming, clever, and a host of other wonderful qualities. Without us ADD-ers, the world would be a rather dull, lackluster place. So it only becomes a disorder in the context of the child (or adult) not knowing how to work with his tendency to space out, procrastinate, become easily distracted, and so on.

Unless they are highly motivated or interested in a task, people with slow theta prefrontal activity will find it difficult to get started on mundane activities, making them terrible procrastinators. Children and teens with ADD usually put off doing something unpleasant or boring, often creating a swirl of chaos and drama around them as the household moves into an uproar with parents shouting, "Why do you always leave things to the last minute?" The resulting frenzy acts like a stimulant on the brain, with the adrenalin kicking the prefrontal cortex into high gear so it can focus enough to pull together the last-minute completion of that uninteresting task.

The Hunter and the Farmer
One of the most user-friendly explanations I've come across for ADD is Thom Hartmann's[1] Hunter/Farmer model. After his own son was evaluated and told by a psychiatrist that he had "Minimal Brain Dysfunction" (which is what ADD was called years ago), Thom began thinking about another way of explaining

the issues of impulsivity and distractibility that challenged his boy. Reading an article in *Scientific American* about the shift from hunting to farming societies, he began pondering this question: *What would make for a successful hunter?* As he thought about it, he realized there were a few qualities that would be really good to have if you were going to be a good hunter.

The first: *Distractibility*. There's a rustle in the bushes nearby and, while others might tune it out, you hear it. The second: *Impulsivity*. You hear a rustle in the bushes nearby and, while others might at least thoughtfully consider whether they should go explore what might have caused the noise, you (the hunter) charge off, hardly thinking about it. You're carried along by the impulse that a good hunt may be about to happen.

If you were a *farmer*, you would have different abilities. You wouldn't be very useful at noticing potential food rustling in the bushes like the hunter, but you'd be good at doing repetitive, predictable tasks, like watering your crops with regularity, fertilizing every three weeks right on schedule, and patiently sitting and picking the bugs off your cotton plants hour after hour . . . after hour. The hunter would go nuts doing this, but the farmer manages very well with such steady, plodding, repetitive tasks.

ADHD behaviors as disorders or hunter traits, based on Thom Hartmann's work.

Trait as it appears in the "Disorder" view:	How it appears in the "Hunter" view:	Opposite "Farmer" traits:
Attention span short, but can become intensely focused for long periods of time	Constantly monitoring the environment	Not easily distracted from the task at hand
Poor planner: Disorganized and impulsive (makes snap decisions)	Able to throw self into the chase on a moment's notice	Able to sustain a steady, dependable effort
Distorted sense of time; unaware of how long it will take to do something	Flexible; ready to change strategy quickly	Organized, purposeful. Has a long-term strategy and sticks to it
Impatient	Tireless; capable of sustained drives, but only when "hot on the trail" of some goal	Conscious of time and timing. Gets things done in time, paces self, has good "staying power"
Doesn't convert words into concepts adeptly, and vice versa. May or may not have a reading disability	Visual/Concrete thinker, clearly seeing a tangible goal, even if there are no words for it	Patient. Aware that good things take time; willing to wait
Has difficult following directions	Independent	Team player
Daydreamer	Bored by mundane tasks; enjoys new ideas, excitement, "the hunt," being hot on the trail	Focused. Good at follow-through, tending to details, "taking care of business"
Acts without considering the consequences	Willing and able to take risk and face danger	Careful. "Look before you leap"
Lacking in the social graces	"No time for niceties when there are decisions to be made!"	Nurturing; creates and supports community values; attuned to whether something will last

Where this becomes enormously interesting is when Thom asks: *What kind of environment is school best suited for? A hunter or a farmer?"* Whenever I pose this question to children, they immediately blurt out, "School is easy for farmers and really boring for hunters!" Using the Hunter/Farmer model is one of the best ways I've found to explain ADD to a parent or child in a way that minimizes the disorder aspect and opens the possibilities for working *with* these tendencies to make life in our predominantly "farmer-oriented" world easier to navigate. ADD is like being a hunter in a farmer's world.

Still, even if parents begin rethinking the ADD label and start viewing their disorganized, distractible, impulsive child as a "hunter," they will nonetheless need to help their child with the challenges of living in a world that doesn't look kindly on breaking promises, windows, or arms.

A few suggestions for helping ADD-ish kids

The first approach I take with ADD-ish children (and everything I say is equally applicable to adults with ADD/ ADHD) is to help them begin to notice when they're "here" and when they've "checked out." All change is built upon awareness, so I invite kids to start getting a feel for when they're present—which is where we have to be to absorb or remember something—and when it just *looks* as though they're present.

Parents can help their children build what I refer to as the *muscle* of attention by playing what I call the "Distraction Monster" game. Invite the child to try to focus on a relatively easy homework assignment while you try (gently, at first) to distract them. As they start doing their math problems, Mom would say something out loud like, "I wonder what I should make for dinner? Hmmm, the kids always like rutabagas and Brussels sprouts..." The child does her best to continue with her task and not look up; if she succeeds, she gets a point. If she does look up, Mom gets the point. Kids love having permission to ignore their parents, and this game—especially as it gets more challenging—helps them learn how to harness their attention to stay on task, even when they're tempted to focus elsewhere.

Another game that can help a child increase their attention and focus is to give them a series of fun commands to do, and let them know you will *not* repeat them. "Walk backwards to the backyard, pick up three blades of grass, put them in my left hand, and start singing the Happy Birthday song." Start from simple to more complicated; most kids love to play this, and it gives them a feeling for what it's like to use 100% of their attention.

I also ask parents—and their children—to take a look at lifestyle factors that can either exaggerate or reduce problems with focus and attention. A brain that's well rested, well hydrated, and well nourished is more stable than a brain that's tired, dehydrated, and running on empty calories. I have had clients with serious focusing problems find their attention noticeably improve simply from cutting out sugar and getting adequate sleep.

A 1993 Cornell University study found that eliminating dairy products, wheat, corn, yeast, soy, citrus, eggs, chocolate, peanuts, and artificial colors and preservatives seemed to decrease ADHD symptoms.[3] An earlier study[3] showed that a low-allergen diet supplemented with calcium, magnesium, zinc, and vitamins produced favorable results. Levels of omega-3s in the plasma and red blood cells of children with ADHD are lower than in non-ADHD children, so it may be beneficial to include a daily dose of omega-3s. While many refute claims that foods and additives impact ADHD symptoms, there are at least some who believe that diet and lifestyle changes can make life easier for "hunters."

Homework

Let's talk for a minute about one of the biggest problems for children with (and without) ADD: homework. In addressing this aspect of parenting an ADD-ish child, it's critical that parents come *alongside* the child in a spirit of support and friendliness, communicating that they're on the child's side rather than coming across in an adversarial, threatening way. By understanding what the child is up against when she struggles to stay focused on tasks that hold absolutely no intrinsic, genuine appeal—like doing several math worksheets or copying spelling words—a parent who can say, "I get it, sweetie—this really isn't your thing, is it?" paves the way for the child to be more open to suggestions for getting it done.

I help kids learn how to help their brain wake up before they start homework, by tapping gently all over their skull, or unrolling their outer ears from the top to the bottom. (This helps a child focus by stimulating important acupuncture points.) Another way to help them prepare for a homework session is to spray a scented room freshener where they'll be working. The smell activates their brain without being too distracting.

The Ten Minute Rule is very useful in helping kids do homework they are resisting. It simply involves suggesting to the child that he only perform the unpleasant task for ten minutes, even if it's likely to take longer. After ten minutes, he gets to decide whether to stop or continue on. This is one of my favorite tricks for getting myself to do mundane jobs like filing papers or doing dishes!

Another idea is to have the child do a portion of the assignment and then hop up and down ten times or walk backwards to the front door and back, then resume working. Interrupting the dreaded task with something silly and fun will help wake up that prefrontal cortex and make the homework feel less like a life sentence while awakening their arousal so they can focus better. We want children to be able to see the light at the end of the tunnel, which is accomplished when we break up big assignments into bite-sized, more doable tasks.

Stop caring so much

When my home-schooled son began going to public school in sixth grade, he would dutifully come home, lay his books out on the coffee table, and begin doing his homework. I would ask him, "What are you doing?"

"Homework," looking at me with a fair degree of certainty that he was answering a question with an obvious answer.

"Why are you doing that?"

"Because I have stuff due tomorrow!"

"But you've been in school all day, honey. Why don't

you go out to play for a while?"

Invariably my son would say, "Mom, I have to do my homework, okay?!"

In other words, without me being overly invested in it, or *needing* him to do his homework to quell *my* anxiety, I left him with the psychological space to care about it on his own. To this day, he's extremely conscientious about getting homework done; and while he knows I care very much about how he's doing in school, he also knows I don't *need* him to perform a particular way to feel okay.

By exploring strategies to make the hunter's life in the farmer's world a little easier, we display an understanding of our ADD'ish child's brain and celebrate its unique gifts and contributions to our lives and to the world. Ultimately, we hunters—if equipped with tools to keep us on track—make for fascinating, spontaneous, multifaceted, creative human beings. We just need to get through the farmer's world with our self-respect, passion for learning, and confidence intact. And having parents on our side, guiding us along the way, makes that a likely outcome.

Tips for nurturing the genius in your child

Provide your kids with toys and activities that challenge them in their particular area of talent. Give the Visual/Spatially intelligent child one of the many hands-on, manipulative games on the market today, like Rush Hour or a Rubik's cube. Allow your Naturalist child to wash dogs at the local animal shelter once a month. Let your Interpersonal child volunteer with you at a geriatric center to visit elderly people who will find him engaging, or let him help out with a neighbor's little kids.

If your child is naturally gifted at Logic/Mathematic or Verbal/Linguistic intelligence, school will be easier for her. But don't drop the ball. These kids still need the chance to develop their creative interests. And if your child isn't a natural in math or language arts, be her ally rather than her adversary, as you attempt to help her succeed in the academic world. Be honest with your children about what their grades do—and don't—mean about their intelligence.

If your child claims to be without any drive or passion, take them to the magazine section of a local bookstore and ask them to pick one that captures his attention. The smorgasbord of topics covered in this section can help identify a child's interests, beyond playing video games, watching TV or surfing the Internet.

Most importantly, celebrate this child, and all children, as they are. Be their cheerleader and champion as they travel along their journey towards becoming who they were truly meant to be. Recognize the blessings of their one-of-a-kind uniqueness. Feed their spirit and nurture their talents so they feel empowered to choose life paths that weave in the particular gifts they've been blessed with that nourish their soul.

Questions and Suggestions

Question: *I like the idea of encouraging my children to develop their innate talents and to find professions that capitalize on their natural gifts, but it seems to me it's important that they learn how to do things they don't always consider fun. Don't you think children have to learn to do the dirty work and the tough things that may not come easy to them?*

Suggestion: Absolutely. A child who hasn't learned how to clean a toilet, weed a garden, or write a thank-you letter is at a disadvantage when it comes to thriving in the world. Kids—and adults—need to stretch beyond their comfort zones to keep growing. Playing it safe by only doing the things we're good at is a recipe for stagnation.

My point isn't that we should modify our children's world so they only do the things they love to do, but rather that they deserve to have their interests acknowledged and respected and that they should be given opportunities to develop their natural gifts and passions. A child who has the chance to shine at what he is naturally good at will find that his aliveness spills over into tasks and challenges that would otherwise be more difficult. In other words, when we give our kids the chance to develop their innate talents on a regular basis, their ability to do the hard stuff improves.

***

Question: *As much as I think my son probably has a lot more musical talent than math or language arts, I worry that if I stop leaning on him to do his homework, he'll spend all his time playing drums. Are you suggesting that I let him focus all his free time on music and let his grades take a nosedive?*

Suggestion: Not at all. Even if your son's passion *is* music, it's vital that he experience success at school in the more traditional subjects. If he doesn't do his homework, he'll find it harder and harder to keep up. No child benefits from getting poor grades.

Give your son the extra support he needs to do well in math and language arts. Just make sure you allow him his Wall of Futility moments when he has to stop playing drums to do his homework. If you let him know you're on his side, and refrain from judging and lecturing, he'll be more willing to buck up and do the dreaded math worksheets, *especially if he's also getting time to do what he loves to do.* The enjoyment and confidence he experiences from doing what he enjoys will improve the attitude he brings to doing the things he believes to be unimportant.

As he gets older, you may consider taking him to a college campus so he can start to connect the dots between doing "dumb" homework and getting to go to a cool place like college. You can also introduce him to an older kid who's a drummer *and* a good student. Celebrate his talent, help him express his frustration (Act I) at not being able to do what he loves as much as he'd like, and hold fast to your role as the captain of the ship that he needs to help him stay afloat with his schoolwork.

***

Question: *My wife and I have a very musical and artistic fifth-grade daughter, and she's been miserable at school for a long time. What do you think about home schooling?*

Suggestion: Gosh, this topic could be a book unto itself. Short answer: I home schooled my own son until he entered the sixth grade. Our days were generally unstructured; for instance, I taught him the vowel sounds on the drive into town, and we did math problems as he was falling asleep at night (at his insistence). He played a lot of basketball in the driveway and read a *lot* (including everything ever written about Calvin and Hobbes.) When he went to school at age ten or eleven, he was an A student who scored in the upper 90th percentile of standardized tests.

I'm not saying this to brag about my son—really—or to gloat about how casual I was in my approach to his early education. Looking back, I realize that if I had it to do all over again, there are things I would now do much differently. But my point is that given the relatively minimal amount of formal instruction he received and how well he still did when he went to school, it's clear to me that in most cases we overemphasize the amount of learning that takes place in a typical classroom. Throw in the fact that if a child's natural interests are fed for only an hour or two per week at school and that your daughter's inner spark seems to be dimming, I would certainly recommend you look into home schooling.

Home schooling is *not* for everyone, however. And with a sixth grader, you'll need to have a structured approach to her instruction and perhaps supplement it with some tutoring. If she's a social child and you don't have lots of kids around for her to be with regularly, you'll have to look for gatherings and group activities for home-schooled children, as well as encourage her to be involved in extracurricular activities that capture her interest. There are many home-school conferences and websites available that can point you in the right direction. One company that manages distance learning and does an excellent job is Laurel Springs School, but there are many others.

I am *not* against school. I'm a credentialed teacher and I take education very seriously. My son is a dedicated, Advanced Placement student, and I care very much about how he does in his classes. I simply believe that we've come to a point where it's clear that the institution of school isn't necessarily right for every child. For those who can manage home schooling, it can provide another option for a good education.

Chapter Ten
How to Help Kids Avoid Depression and Anxiety

"Just because a thought shows up doesn't mean you need to make it a sandwich."
Susan Stiffelman

"I hate my life. . . . Nobody likes me. . . . I just know I'm going to get an F on this report." Kids can be notoriously black-and-white thinkers. A thought shows up in their head—perhaps prompted by a bit of evidence that might support it—and they adamantly believe it's true. Often, they've observed negative or anxiety-producing thought patterns in their parents, making them less than receptive when Mom or Dad tries to talk cheer them up or talk them out of their catastrophic thinking. In addition, there might be a genetic predisposition towards disregulation, which, when combined with hormones, poor diet, lack of sleep, and/or difficulties with friends or school, can send a teen or younger child into a downward spiral.

According to the FDA, in 2003 more than ten million antidepressant prescriptions were dispensed to patients younger than eighteen years of age; that number grows higher every year. At any given time, one in every thirty-three children may have clinical depression; the rate for adolescents may be as high as one in eight[1]. Suicide is the third-leading cause of death for fifteen- to twenty-four-year-olds and the sixth-leading cause of death for children between the ages of five and fifteen[2]. About thirteen percent of children and adolescents ages nine to seventeen experience some kind of anxiety disorder.

Depression and anxiety are debilitating conditions. It's important that parents not dismiss their child's chronic sadness or worry as merely being the result of changing hormones or fatigue. While my approaches to these two conditions will overlap, I'm going to address them separately before I offer some general guidelines.

If you suspect your child suffers from depression, anxiety, or any other mood disorder, please seek professional help. This chapter is not meant to be an exhaustive explanation about mood disorders in children. It is only a very general look at some of the ways parents can help children be less vulnerable to some of the forces that can send them tumbling emotionally.

Depression

Sadness is a natural response to loss or grief, and it's a normal emotion for children and teens; but if sadness becomes persistent and/or interferes with a child's normal functioning, parents need to take action. It's important to know some of the signs of depression in children and adolescents and to recognize the difference between occasional sadness and true depression. If a child has a number of these symptoms for two weeks or more, parents should pursue appropriate help.

While it's very possible that a youngster's low-grade depression is a passing phase, it is vital that parents rule out a more serious mood disorder. Remember that children who are depressed won't necessarily appear to have these symptoms all the time. Most importantly, if your instincts tell you something's wrong, pay attention. If your gut tells you that your child is in trouble, seek outside guidance, regardless of whether or not your concerns seem rational. And any comment a child or adolescent makes that suggests he is thinking about suicide ("I wish I were dead" or "You'd all be better off without me") must be taken extremely seriously by parents, who should seek trusted professional assistance immediately.

> For parents to have real influence over a child or teen's bout with depression, they first need to ensure that the child is going to be willing to talk openly about the challenges she's going through.

Much of the time a child's depression will come on slowly and can be addressed, and often curtailed, if parents help their child deal effectively with underlying factors. This might involve helping her implement lifestyle changes—including improved diet and sleep—as well as cognitive approaches for dealing with the thoughts and beliefs that often precipitate a downward spiral. But for parents to have real influence over a child or teen's bout with depression, they first need to ensure that they are willing to let her talk openly about the challenges she's going through.

Parents need to make it clear to their youngsters that they are *capable* of hearing their bad news without minimizing it, dismissing them, or talking them out of their dark feelings and emotions. For a child or teen to tell his parents about his troubles, he needs to know that they are capable of hearing him out without falling apart or trying to fix things or cheer him up. If a youngster is depressed, what he initially needs most is to feel that his parents will hear and understand him (Act I); then they can figure out how to help him feel better (Act II)

When the parent-child relationship is fragile, the prospect of turning to Mom or Dad can seem daunting to a troubled youngster. Oftentimes, the child or teen who is struggling with depression feels very alone. A depressed youngster's thinking can be distorted, and her low mood dampens her motivation to do much of anything, including reaching out for help. It behooves every parent to strengthen the connection with their children or adolescents so they can maintain a climate that lets them offload the upsets from difficult patches along the road of growing up, learning how to avoid becoming habituated to lethargy and malaise as a way of coping with life challenges.

Anxiety

I'm struck by what I see as increasingly escalating levels of anxiety in the teens and children I work with. Despite having their basic needs taken care of and living in relatively safe circumstances (if you don't count earthquakes, fires, and mudslides, that is) many children—at ever-younger ages—are tormented by worry and fear. I'm not referring to ordinary childhood fears, which are normal and expected. Nor am I discounting legitimate fears based on actual trauma. Children who have experienced true calamity need proper care and attention to help them heal, which often includes counseling by a qualified professional.

I'm referring here to chronic anxiety, fueled by worrisome thinking that prevents a child from falling asleep, keeps him from participating in regular activities, or distracts him throughout his day. As my son would say, "What's up with that?" What's going on in our children's lives that promotes such widespread anxiety?

I'm not suggesting this is something altogether new. I come from a long line of worriers, and I know that many of us have worry imprinted—often in flashing neon lights—onto our DNA. But the level of fear I see in children today is often pervasive and paralyzing. Our children need to grow up with the deep sense that they're safe.

Perhaps it's a result of living in an increasingly scary world, images of which are easily accessed on the Internet or on TV. Terrorism is no longer a vague concept; children are growing up accustomed to walking through metal detectors and cautioned to remain on alert for "suspicious activity" when they travel, Our kids hear about school shootings on the news, and see magazine covers that shout out headlines about kidnappings and rapes. Add to this the fact that many anxious children are highly sensitive. They pick up on their parents' distress, often magnifying it.

Anxiety is not inherently a bad thing. It's a normal reaction to new or stressful situations. Anxiety signals the body to prepare for action in the face of danger, and it causes us to be careful, pay attention, or prepare to solve a problem. It also helps children learn to obey rules and develop a conscience.

Physical symptoms include rapid breathing, muscle tension, "butterflies" in the stomach, racing heart, and feeling tired. Psychological symptoms include worried thoughts, obsessive fears, and perfectionism. Other symptoms of anxiety in children include clinginess, tearfulness, physical complaints, irritability, tantrums, and inflexibility. When these symptoms interfere with a child or teen's daily life—preventing her from participating in social events or classes, or making it difficult for her to fall asleep—we would say that the anxiety has become a problem.

A chronically anxious child can be very tiring to deal with. She doesn't do well with changes in schedule, new experiences, or unplanned events where her fears might be activated. Her imagination of potential danger or harm triggers actual physiological symptoms—racing heart, sweaty palms and the like, which immobilize her from stepping into the unknown. Parents often lose their cool as they find themselves almost imprisoned by the anxious child's rigid need for control, routine, and reassurance.

You may have guessed by now that the first thing I do with the parents of an anxious child is to help them deal with their own frustration if it's impairing their ability to understand their child's experience without judgment and irritation. As I've said, anxious kids are usually quite sensitive, so a parent's exasperation or impatience can fuel their apprehension and make it worse. Parents who get a feeling for why—from the child's vantage point—he *should* need them to check under his bed five times before he goes to sleep, are in a position to better comfort the child and walk him through the irrationality of his fears and obsessions. (For more on this, read about The Four Questions in Chapter 1.)

Little Fear Guy
One way I talk about anxiety with children is by introducing them to "Little Fear Guy." I tell them that Little Fear Guy sits on their shoulder and is dedicated to their safety. I explain that LFT isn't their enemy, but he often thinks they're in more danger than they really are. (I picture my Little Fear Guy as Barney Fife from the *Andy Griffith Show*, who routinely gets everyone in town stirred up about some imagined danger.) Little Fear Guy can exaggerate things or get kids worked up and nervous when they're actually quite safe. One of my anxious young clients told me her Little Fear Guy drank a lot of Red Bull!

By objectifying the source of their worry-generator and recognizing it as a well-intentioned, but not always accurate voice in their head, children feel more empowered to update Little Fear Guy with information that might lessen his belief that their survival is at risk. LFG allows kids to *de-personalize* their thoughts. Rather than asking a worried child, "What are *you* afraid of?" I ask, "What is *Little Fear Guy* whispering—or shouting—in your ear?"

By using Little Fear Guy, it's easier for an anxious child to have some distance from the thoughts that often precipitate their unfounded or distorted fears.

Shapeless versus Specific Fear

I also talk to children about *shapeless* fear versus *specific* fear. Shapeless fear just makes us globally afraid. If you ask a child with shapeless fears around going to a sleepover to explain what they're anxious about, they with simply say, "I don't know! I'm just scared!" Shapeless fear is pervasive and powerful, and causes children to feel victimized by their worries.

I recently worked with a youngster who found it impossible to approach a teacher to ask if he could change study groups in one of his classes. He got nervous and his palms got sweaty if he even thought about talking to his teacher; approaching him was simply too frightening to consider. As we talked, I got him to describe the worst-case scenario, the most awful thing that might happen if he talked to his teacher. When we started to make his fear *specific*—"The teacher might say no, or he might crack a joke about how my current group couldn't make it without me"—he discovered the grip of fear had loosened considerably. A week or two later he came in smiling, telling me he'd finally asked Mr. S. He went on to tell me, "He told me I couldn't change my group." I whooped it up anyway, applauding and high-fiving him with great enthusiasm. He laughed, saying, "But did you hear me? He said 'No!' He's not letting me change groups."

"I don't care," I told him. "You did it! You worked around the limits Little Fear Guy was laying on you! You broke out of jail! Pat yourself on the back!"

By coming *alongside* anxious children as they express their fear, we can help reduce its effects. In addition, when parents model calmness in the face of uncertainty, it profoundly influences children to do the same. The more your kids see you handling potentially worrisome events in a confident, relaxed way, the more they will be influenced to reconsider how dangerous something actually is—or isn't.

What follows is an approach I took in working with a depressed youngster named Daniel. Many of the things I did also apply to working with a child who is anxious. As an aside, I frequently see youngsters who struggle with both depression *and* anxiety, which often go hand in hand.

Daniel's depression

Daniel had been a relatively easy child to raise. As he approached ninth grade, however, some of the kids he had been friendly with since grammar school began experimenting with pot and alcohol. Daniel wasn't interested in joining in, but given his fairly shy personality, he didn't feel confident about finding new friends and often felt isolated and lonely.

In addition to having emotional stress in his life, Daniel was often running on fumes. As is often the case with teens, he found himself wide-awake at ten o'clock, often staying up till midnight or one in the morning. In addition, he had never been much of a breakfast eater, so he often left for school deprived of sleep, short on food, and feeling an ever-worsening gloom as each school day began. Just keeping it together to get through classes and maintain his schoolwork was exhausting. By the time Daniel got home at the end of the day, he was tired and grumpy; he ended up hiding out in his room much of the evening.

Daniel's parents noticed him staying home more often on weekends and asked him why he wasn't spending time with his old friends. Given his prior experience with his parents—they generally focused on cheering him up when he was upset rather than hearing him out—he felt it would be pointless to tell them what was going on with his buddies, so he offered excuses about how his old friends were busy with other things. Daniel slept much of the weekends; his parents chalked it up to adolescence. He became more moody and irritable; his folks attributed it to hormones. He played video games for hours, becoming very edgy whenever he had to turn them off; his parents assumed this was normal teen behavior. After several months, Daniel's grades began slipping. His parents, finally unable to deny that something was wrong in Daniel's life, called me for a consultation.

My first task was to help this family open up the channels of communication. The truth is a powerful thing. I knew that if we could create a safe space for Daniel to tell his parents what he was going through—and have them receive it in a way that encouraged him to keep talking—we could help this young man receive the support he so badly needed from his mom and dad. I began working with his folks, Jeff and Kyra, to help them restore their roles as captains of the ship in their son's life. I also spent time with Daniel, who was in need of a place to offload his sadness and pain.

In light of other factors—including a family history of depression—I got Daniel to agree to go for a medical workup so that I could be assured we had ruled out medical conditions that might have been contributing to his depression. With a clean bill of health, I worked with him in a number of ways, including convincing him to modify his schedule so he could get more sleep, and figuring out some foods he was willing to eat in the morning so he was nourished before his school day began.

For those of you with teens, you may be wondering how I enlisted his willingness to shift his sleep and diet. As with all the work I do, I started by coming *alongside* Daniel and listening without judgment as he explained his desire to stay up late and his lack of appetite in the morning. Because he perceived me as being on his side rather than trying to force an agenda on him about sleep and food, he and I together came up with some reasonable shifts that he felt good about and that he didn't feel had been force on him.

Although lifestyle changes were a part of the picture, one of the big shifts I hoped to help Daniel make had to do with the thoughts that were perpetuating his depressed state. He told me that when he wasn't distracted by TV or video games at home, or class work at school, he felt extremely lonely and self-conscious. He confessed to believing that kids thought he was a geek, and he was embarrassed about not having friends to hang around with, especially at lunchtime.

I found out that Jeff and Kyra often said things in front of him like, "We're probably going to miss our flight" or "I just know the tournament is going to be rained out." Having learned negative thinking patterns from his parents, Daniel was limited in his ability to question the irrational but powerful thoughts that triggered his belief that he couldn't make new friends. I introduced all three family members to methods of questioning and challenging their automatic negative thinking patterns.

Using The Four Questions

Using the Four Questions and the Turnarounds (introduced in Chapter 1), Daniel was able to take an honest look at the thoughts and assumptions that brought on his sense of aloneness. One of the thoughts he frequently believed was "Nobody likes me." Daniel surprised his parents by how quickly he understood the strategy of Turnaround, and he was able to almost effortlessly find evidence to contradict his negative beliefs, which led him to realize that his belief that no one liked him had influenced him to appear aloof to kids who might otherwise try to become his friend.

I explained that by shining a big, bright light on our thoughts, we see them for what they are. One analogy I use is from the *Wizard of Oz*. Dorothy and her companions have finally made it to Oz and are standing in front of the great wizard—at least the projection of him, booming voice and all. As they stand there trembling, little Toto the dog runs off. When Dorothy finds him, he's using his teeth to pull back the curtain of a tiny booth, behind which sits the actual Wizard of Oz, a harmless little man pulling levers and amplifying his voice through a microphone. In the same way that the Wizard of Oz loomed large and seemed so intimidating, sometimes our thoughts seem to carry truths that in the end are insignificant, untrue notions that had wormed their way into our minds.

ABC thinking

Another approach I taught Daniel and his parents is called "ABC thinking." "A"—the *actual* event, as it would be impartially reported on by an uninvolved observer; "B"—the *belief* about the event, or our judgment or interpretation of it; and "C"—the *consequence* of our believing what we believed in "B." Using this strategy, I was able to help Daniel and his parents observe the ways they often misinterpreted people's behavior and external events. "Sometimes the belief or interpretation we give to something is simply wrong, but instead of challenging it, we buy into it. As a consequence, we feel bad, worried, angry, or hurt. I call this a case of having the "Bad B's!"

I illustrated with an example: "Let's say your teacher quickly glances at a report you've worked on, and doesn't say anything. "A" might be, 'My teacher got the report and made no comment.' You would simply describe what happened, without embellishing. Now let's say you end up feeling upset. We might say your "C" would be, 'I feel worried about what kind of grade he's going to give me.' What might the Bad "B" be that would lead you to feel that way?" Daniel responded by saying, "I guess my Bad "B" might be, 'He took one look at it and thought it was too short' or 'He's already decided I didn't do a good job.'"

"That's right, Daniel. Those would be the Bad "B's" that would leave you feeling bad. But the truth is, you *aren't* a mind reader, and you *don't* know what he was thinking when he glanced at your paper." I encouraged Daniel and his folks to create some *good* "B's" that might be equally true—or even truer than his Bad "B's," and might lead him to feel better rather than worse. With a little help, Daniel was able to come up with some alternative "B's." "Maybe he only glanced at the report because he wants to read it without me standing there, or he might have just glanced at it quickly because he's distracted by other things." These "B's" would leave Daniel feeling just fine rather than worried or discouraged.

As Daniel's parents began learning how to question their own negative thinking, they were able to help Daniel apply these tools in real-life situations. He began to learn how to avoid buying into the beliefs that caused him to feel unlikable and alone. By learning to loosen the grip of the stories that arrived uninvited in his mind, Daniel began noticing the ways kids at school were showing an interest in him that he had previously overlooked. As Daniel's mom and dad became their son's allies in his struggle with depression, he discovered how good it felt to turn to them for comfort and support.

Airplanes, thoughts, and sandwiches

In one of my sessions with Daniel and his parents, I described thoughts as tiny little airplanes that fly around our heads. "If a thought shows up in our head—like 'No one likes me'—and we don't create a place for that thought/airplane to land, it buzzes out and leaves us alone. But if that thought arrives in our head and we start waving our arms saying, 'Land here! I have a great landing strip for you!' then that thought settles into our mind and parks itself. We then start believing the thought is correct and looking for evidence and proof to support its truth."

I went on to give one of my favorite analogies: "Imagine that a scruffy, smelly guy off the street walks into your house, goes into your kitchen, opens your fridge, and pops open a can of soda. He then wanders into the master bedroom, settles himself in the bed, grabs the remote, and starts watching TV while he sips his drink. Would you walk in and ask him, 'Would you like a sandwich with that?' or would you say, 'Get out of my house!'?"

Daniel and his folks smiled, and his mom voiced what all of them were thinking: "We'd definitely tell him to get out!"

I smiled and continued, "Well, this is sort of what we need to do with thoughts. When a thought shows up that has the power to make us sad, angry, or anxious, we don't *have* to believe it or politely listen while it drones on with its dreary monologue. We can question the thinking that led us to whatever fuels our bad feelings, and we can jump off that train of negative thought *before* it arrives at its gloomy destination. *Just because a thought shows up doesn't mean you need to make it a sandwich!*"

In the end, Daniel and his parents came to feel grateful that his struggle with depression began—and ended—while he was still young. The tools he learned to use to lessen the effect of his negative thinking served him in years to come as his school load got heavier. And the habits of eating well, exercising, and making sure he got adequate sleep were of enormous help when he faced the bigger challenges of life as a college student.

> When a thought shows up that has the power to make us sad, or angry, or anxious, *we don't have to believe it.*

There was a time in the not-too-distant past when depression and anxiety were hidden, and there was a stigma attached to someone who struggled with maintaining mental balance and well-being. Today's children are fortunate be growing up at a time when we no longer have to pretend we're okay; our kids are learning to redefine true strength as having the ability to ask for—and receive—help when we need it.

Parents who become aware that their child or teen is suffering emotionally are giving their child an important gift when they invite her to tell the truth about her struggles and show her that they're there to help her out of her dark hole. This doesn't mean parents instantly fix every problem, but it does mean they walk by her side as she finds her way back to her joy. By equipping a child or teen with the tools to help her avoid getting stuck in the cycle of depression and anxiety, parents give their child an essential leg up toward living a successful, satisfying life.

Steps to take if you suspect your teen or younger child is depressed

> Make sure the relationship you have with your child is strong and that he feels a natural comfort with confiding in you.

> Give your child the clear impression that you can handle whatever she tells you, so she doesn't feel she has to protect you from her bad news.

> When your child does tell you his problems—big or small ones—listen openly. Do not try to fix things right away or talk him out of his feelings or perceptions.

> If your instincts suggest that your child is depressed or in trouble, pay attention and get reliable, outside help.

> If your child or teen demonstrates a number of the aforementioned signs of depression for more than two weeks, get outside help.

> Include a medical workup for a teen or younger child with depression to rule out any possible physical causes.

> Ensure your youngster is getting adequate sleep and exercise and is following a reasonably nutritious diet.

Be mindful of what your child observes you doing when you are disappointed or discouraged.

Learn—and help your child learn—strategies for challenging the negative thoughts and interpretations that precipitate depression.

Questions and Suggestions

Question: *My seven-year-old daughter worries about everything. She worries about her Daddy if he doesn't walk in the door by 6:30 at night, she worries that I'm going to forget to pick her up from school, and she worries that she's going to lose me every time we go to the grocery store! My husband and I have tried all kinds of ways of reassuring her, but nothing works and I'm worn-out by her incessant demands and inflexibility. What can I do?*

Suggestion: I've met many children like your daughter; you are not alone. The first step to take is to see if you can reduce your frustration by looking at the thoughts that trigger your resistance to her behavior. I am not for one minute saying it wouldn't frustrate me, too, and I understand how worn-out you are by her constant worrying. I'm just inviting you to face whatever beliefs are making it even harder for you to deal effectively with this situation.

Let's say the upsetting thought is *My daughter shouldn't be afraid that I will forget to pick her up from school.* No doubt, you have mountains of evidence to neutralize her fear and probably have reminded her many times of how groundless her worry is. Even if you were late once or twice, chances are that explaining why these were exceptions—or reminding her that she was still picked up from school—won't alleviate her concern. An anxious child's fears are not based on logic. But if you resist her worries, you'll be less able to help her through them.

What opposite thought could you come up with that would soften your irritation around this worry of hers? Can you come up with three reasons why she *should* be afraid that you'll forget to pick her up? It may sound silly, but our goal is simply to loosen the grip your belief has on you that prevents you from helping your daughter feel less fearful. You may come up with things like, "She saw something on TV about a child whose mother didn't pick her up and who had to walk home in the dark," or "She knows a boy in her grade whose mother got sick and thought another mom got the message to pick him up, only to find he sat there for an hour alone and waiting."

If you can come *alongside* her, you have a better chance of coming up with a solution that helps her feel empowered. I would encourage you to help her create an arm's length from the voice in her head that creates her worries by using Little Fear Guy. You might say, "I notice you worry a lot, honey, when you don't see me in the pickup line at school. What is Little Fear Guy whispering—or shouting—in your ear about that?"

Let's say your daughter replies with, "Little Fear Guy tells me you're going to forget to come and get me."

Instead of saying, "What a silly thing to be worried about!" ask her what happens for her when she thinks that thought. "When you believe that, honey, where do you feel scared? In your tummy? In your hands?" I try to help my anxious clients get more connected to what they're experiencing in their bodies, such as belly/chest breathing or progressive relaxation when she's getting agitated (see Chapter 11).

You might also use ABC thinking in this situation, helping her learn that when she has a worry based on something unlikely, she can see it as a case of the "Bad B's!" Kids enjoy playing around with whatever the Belief was in response to the Actual event that brought them a particular Consequence.

Be careful about promoting her fears by turning on your "Mom TV" and engaging in long, dramatic discussions about her worries that go nowhere and inadvertently create a payoff for her to perpetuate them. Instead, give her room to feel and name her fears without trying to use logic to convince her that her concerns are ridiculous. Instead, help your daughter examine the thoughts and beliefs that trigger her distress.

As the captain of the ship, if you reduce *your* anxiety about *her* anxiety, you'll be able to help your little girl learn to manage her fears, learning a vital skill along the way.

***

Question: *I suspect that one of the reasons my son is so anxiety-prone is that I'm a worrier and always have been. I try to say the right things to comfort him when he starts fretting about something, but the truth is, I don't think I'm very convincing. How can I help him when I don't believe the reassuring things I say to him?*

Suggestion: If you've got your own Little Fear Guy issues, it can be difficult to not have him affect the help you offer your anxious son!

I urge you to use the Four Questions around your worrisome thoughts on a regular basis. Look for whatever idea or belief seems to trigger the onslaught of negative thoughts, and move through the four questions and turnaround to diffuse the affect. If there are other elements contributing to your anxiety— too much stress, too little sleep, biochemical imbalances—make sure you take steps to address them. By modeling for your son the effort you're making to take charge of Little Fear Guy, you'll show him—without saying a thing—that we don't need to live fearfully in the prison he often creates for us.

While it's natural that, as a parent, you'd want to say comforting things to your son when he's distressed, your words will be overshadowed by your emotional state. A child's radar is extremely accurate. Until you work with genuinely *being* less worried, the reassuring things you say won't be terribly effective. Start working to take charge of Little Fear Guy, and you'll be in a position to help your son when he's anxious.

***

Question: *We have a lot of depression and addiction issues in our family. Are there steps I can follow to help protect my daughter from becoming depressed?*

Suggestion: Yes, most definitely. While it's beyond the scope of this book to answer this question with specifics, I would encourage you to make sure you're providing your child with a few things. First, you can help her express her feelings rather than bottling them up, which is an essential aspect of avoiding depression. Help your daughter develop language to express her emotions. Make sure her diet is healthy and nourishing; I recommend information put out by Dr. Daniel Amen and Dr. Andrew Weil, and there are many other reliable sources for ideas in this area.

Help your daughter learn to pay attention to and acknowledge the positive things in her life. A recent *Scientific*

American[3] article described a study by Simons and Chabris in which subjects were told to count the number of times a group of basketball players passed the ball to one another in a sixty-second period. The task required tremendous concentration, since the ball moved so quickly. During the sixty seconds, someone who was dressed in a gorilla suit walked through the players, faced the viewers, thumped his chest and left. To the amazement of the researchers, half the viewers failed to notice the gorilla! Their conclusion was that things that don't fit our predetermined script are simply deleted from our awareness. This powerful experiment points to the truth that we often overlook the wonderful things in our lives when we become habituated to only seeing the negative.

So, help your daughter understand the role her thinking plays in maintaining a positive outlook on life. In addition, ensure that your youngster gets plenty of sleep and lots of exercise; both are critical to helping with depression. Having healthy relationships and connections are also very important.

Genetics is only one predictor of depression. By being proactive, your child has a great chance to avoid depression and the addictive behaviors that it can fuel.

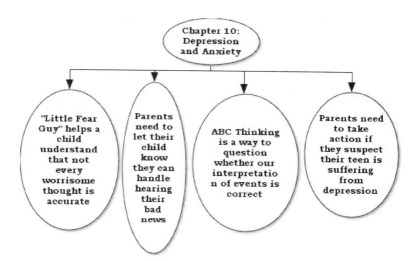

Chapter 10: Depression and Anxiety

"Little Fear Guy" helps a child understand that not every worrisome thought is accurate

Parents need to let their child know they can handle hearing their bad news

ABC Thinking is a way to question whether our interpretation of events is correct

Parents need to take action if they suspect their teen is suffering from depression

Chapter Eleven
Being Present, Mindful, and Unwinding Without Electricity

"I can do several things at once," I said proudly.
"Yes," she replied. "But can you just do one?"

My son (then fourteen) and I were getting ready for lunch on Ngamba Island in Uganda. Nelson, who looked after the guests, collected us for dinner from the platform where we had been sitting and watching orphaned chimpanzees rescued by the Jane Goodall Foundation and offered sanctuary on this island in the middle of Lake Victoria. We arrived at the dining tent, and Noah, the cook, came out to greet us. We'd only been in Africa a few days, but I'd found I was painfully aware of something about myself with which I'm still a bit uncomfortable: my ability to simply be.

Noah was looking at me. His beautiful eyes had a quiet about them, and he was . . . well, he was *present*. As he talked about lunch and smiled so kindly, it was unmistakable: He wasn't doing anything else. He was just there, fully present with us, describing what he'd prepared for our meal. I could feel the quiet in his mind, and I wanted what he had.

Nearly everyone we met in Africa had this sense of inhabiting the moment. When they were eating, they seemed to just be eating. When we were engaged in conversation, they were clearly listening. They seemed to take great pleasure in looking out over a landscape or relaxing after a meal, unhurriedly enjoying the moments as they unfolded.

I felt awkward at first, embarrassed by how difficult it was for me to do the same. The longer we were in Africa, the more aware I became of my mind's perennial motion. But eventually I started to feel the wheels slowing down. I felt much more myself—more human.

The human brain is magnificently designed, having served our species well for thousands of years. We have exceptional capacities for surviving and thriving in a natural environment. The problem is, contemporary society makes demands on us that our nervous systems simply haven't caught up with. One of the byproducts of attempting to adapt to the onslaught of information that comes at us from our TVs, computers, and cell phones (often simultaneously) is increased anxiety, restlessness, and ever-shorter attention spans.

Never have we witnessed such a plethora of problems with attention and impulse issues in children, with approximately 2.5 million being medicated for ADD.[1] As many as one in ten young people may have an anxiety disorder.[2] And the ability to unwind naturally—without some electronic distraction or a substance (legal or not)—is practically a thing of the past. Even the three-year-old child of a friend I was driving after was unhappy when his DVD player ran out of batteries. I suggested he look out the window at the ocean, and he said, "No!" By bombarding our children with the level of stimulation that's beginning to pass as "normal," we're literally retraining their nervous systems to be unable to cope with the natural rhythms of ordinary life.

One of the core requirements for contentment is the ability to be at peace with our circumstances, our environment, and ourselves. We may have acquired ever more sophisticated ways to be entertained, but in the process we've lost the ability to be still and unwind naturally. When children observe their parents relaxing by having a drink, channel surfing or merging with the Internet, they too become agitated, fidgety, and "bored" when there's nothing to distract them from themselves.

In his book *In Praise of Slowness* Carl Honore[3] says, "Fast is busy, controlling, aggressive, hurried, analytical, stressed, superficial, impatient, active, quantity-over-quality. Slow is the opposite: calm, careful, receptive, still, intuitive, unhurried, patient, reflective, quality-over-quantity. It is about making real and meaningful connections—with people, culture, work, food, everything."

While many think of childhood as carefree, the pace at which we hustle our kids is creating increasing stress and anxiety on children at ever-younger ages ("Hurry up! Get in the car! We're going to be late for school/karate/the birthday party/Grandma's!"). Kids are showing the same symptoms of chronic stress as their parents, including sleep difficulties, frequent stomachaches and headaches, and general irritability.

Childhood is brief enough as it is. It's incumbent upon parents to allow their children to move through their days at a pace that's sane. True enjoyment is experienced only in the present. When we live in this moment—not the past or the future—we have within our grasp an indescribable smorgasbord of joy and appreciation. As Eckhart Tolle[4] has said, "Most people treat the present moment as if it were an obstacle that they need to overcome. Since the present moment is Life itself, it is an insane way to live."

So how do you teach your children to savor life moment by moment? It starts with living mindfully in your daily life. By modeling calming behavior for your children—taking a peaceful walk after dinner instead of turning on the TV, or working a jigsaw puzzle on the kitchen table instead of channel surfing—parents offer their kids a template for learning to unwind from a culture moving at a frenetic pace.

When many kids are finished with homework and after-school activities, they gravitate towards the trance offered by television, the stimulation of texting or surfing the Internet, or the sense of power that comes from video games. In the name of providing them with the latest and greatest toys and devices, we're contributing to their inability to be comfortable without having something to hold their attention. More and more children dislike reading; it's becoming increasingly difficult for kids to take pleasure in books or stories because it requires them to *picture* the story unfolding in their mind's eye, which isn't easy when you've gotten used to having the picturing done for you. In a sense, we're turning our kids onto drugs (TV, computer, video games), getting them addicted, and then complaining when they have short attention spans or when they insist they can't live without the latest, greatest electronic distraction. It's my earnest belief that the rampant diagnosis of ADHD in today's society is at least in part a reflection of the stimulation and hectic pace we have adapted for our children.

Researchers at the University of Illinois[5] discovered that symptoms of ADHD were reduced when children spent time in ordinary "green" settings—trees, parks, and grassy backyards. Their results weren't linked to simply giving hyperactive kids the chance to burn off pent-up energy; kids who struggled with attention but had no issues of hyperactivity demonstrated equal improvement in focus and impulse control. The study built on the researchers' previous finding that fewer reports of domestic violence and stronger neighborhood ties were linked to adding grass and trees to the grounds of public housing developments.

I realized early on that the best way to help my son learn how to be present and unwind naturally was to let him observe me living that way. I have always spent time every day meditating; even when my son was very small, he knew Mommy had her bit of time to enjoy being quiet and still. It's so much a part of my life that it's never seemed anything but normal to him that for a little while every day I'm off to spend time drinking in the beauty of my inner world. For you, it might mean that your daughter finds you quietly sitting at the window, relaxed and enjoying the scene outside. Or it could be that she sees you lingering over a cup of tea and really *drinking it in*, not only practically, but sensually. For others, the way they unwind and come back to themselves might be to sit down and play the piano for a while.

Our children also learn about being present by how we interact with them. When your son is telling you something important and you focus on him—ignoring your cell phone if it rings—he's getting a powerful message that being mindful means paying attention to what you're doing while you're doing it. When you invite your daughter to play UNO or go for a walk without being frantic to rush home to get something "useful" checked off your list, you show her the importance of unstructured time. If you notice your "monkey mind" jumping ahead or off to the side when you're with your kids, patiently bring it back to the present moment.

Spending time connecting or playing with our children and listening to them as they offload the worries and problems of their day does wonders for helping them learn to manage stress and anxiety. We so often converse out of the corners of our mouths, half-participants in the dance of connection, uncomfortable with the intimacy that comes when we devote one hundred percent of our attention to the person in front of us.

> We so often converse out of the corners of our mouths, half-participants in the dance of connection, uncomfortable with the intimacy that comes when we devote one hundred percent of our attention to the person in front of us.

It's easy to proclaim how important it is to enjoy our children as they grow up. But, as in other areas of our lives, there's often a difference between what we say and how we actually live, moment to moment. How often do we actually put the brakes on—shutting off our computers and Blackberries—and truly make ourselves available to be with our children without being focused on getting something accomplished?

Learning to follow your breath is one of the quickest ways to come back to *this* moment and reconnect to the present. UCLA's Mindful Awareness Research Center[6] has seen enormous improvements in children with ADHD and other learning issues, not to mention general anxiety and behavioral issues, when these children have learned techniques for staying present. All children benefit from learning ways to slow down naturally, regardless of whether they have a particular problem or challenge. At the end of this chapter I've included some games you can play with your kids that will help all of you stay more in the present.

Zack's family and their busy lives

Zack could be called your typical eleven-year-old. He is his parents' oldest child (and only boy), and they had provided him with the latest in video games and electronic gadgets. His parents came to consult with me because it seemed their son was starting to fall in with what they called "less-desirable" kids. In addition, he seemed angry a lot of the time and was often sarcastic and edgy with his folks.

Both parents were quite busy and very good at juggling many things at once, Michael in his work as a film producer, and

Karen as a stay-at-home mom with many outside hobbies and interests. Their days were tightly scheduled; and although they tried to sit down together at dinner, it seemed the majority of their interactions had to do with getting Zack to accomplish various tasks or chores. "Did you do your homework yet? Have you fed the dog? Why are you still on the computer?" They confessed that it felt as though their household was in constant motion, very task-oriented, and that any sense of relaxation and connectedness seemed to be minimal at best.

I encouraged Zack's parents to shift some of the ways they engaged with their son. "Try simply offering Zack a friendly smile as you're walking through the room where he's watching TV or doing homework. Or sit down beside him when he isn't expecting it and tell him a joke. Say 'I love you' at random moments, or give him a quick back rub. If he tells you something, listen with a quiet mind." I explained to Karen and Michael that when a parent spends time or initiates conversation with their child spontaneously and wholeheartedly—not just because the child demands it—it does more for his self-esteem than all the heartfelt lectures or enrichment classes in the world.

Some interesting things began to happen with Zack. Karen reported that soon after our session she found Zack mindlessly watching TV one afternoon. She came to sit beside him, and he immediately began to get sarcastic and said, "I know, I know. You're about to tell me to do my homework or that my mind is going to rot from watching this stuff."

"Nope! I wasn't thinking any of that, Zack. I just came to say 'Howdy.'" She smiled warmly at him and then went to sit in another part of the room by the window, becoming engrossed in watching her dogs playing outside.

She explained to me, "Zack seemed kind of confused! First he kept glancing up at me; I hate to admit it, but it isn't often that he sees his mom doing nothing like that. I'm always on the go, getting things done. But after a few minutes he spontaneously got up to came to sit with me. We both ended up watching the dogs for a while together, and finally we went outside to play fetch with them. I couldn't believe how willing he was to join me!"

Zack's dad had his own stories to report. One thing he was especially pleased about was what had happened when he drove his son to a friend's house. Michael confessed that he usually fired up the radio on their car rides. This time he refrained, and instead challenged Zack to solve a riddle. (Dad had actually looked online for a few riddles, so he was prepared!) Zack copped an attitude, said he wasn't into stupid riddles, and fell silent. Michael didn't push but instead gave his son the space to sulk. After a few minutes (which Michael said felt like hours) Zack suddenly blurted out the answer. Michael was genuinely astonished, and in his delight he pulled the car over and gave his boy a big hug. Zack was caught off guard and apparently was quite touched. They ended up spending another fifteen minutes or so by the side of the road solving all the riddles Michael had come up with, and then some that they had each heard in the past.

When I next saw Karen and Michael, they felt they were on their way to getting their son back. Both of them acknowledged how determined they were to slow down and be more present with one another and with their son, confessing how difficult it was to avoid checking their phones for "urgent" emails and text messages. Karen actually signed up for a Mindfulness seminar; she was looking forward to developing more of a sense of being present for her own enrichment, as well as to help her model living more in the moment for her children. When I saw her some months later, she had learned a lot about being more mindful and had shown her husband and kids some exercises that helped them all be more present in their interactions with one another.

"Where are you going?"

Much of the time when I show up in my son's room while he's reading or playing guitar, I'm ignored. "Just came to say hi," I say. After sitting a moment or two, I get up to leave. But more often than not, as I'm heading out he says, "Where are you going?" or "Don't go." He wants to be connected. He just needs me to make the first move and to make it clear that I'm available and present for a while, not just there with an agenda or to offer a parenting sound bite.

Not long ago I was helping a young friend do some math. This child is vibrant and alive, and I love spending time with her. As she was scribbling on her paper, she said, "I love the sound the pencil makes on the paper." I was absolutely enchanted by her enjoyment of such a simple thing. I got another pencil and we compared the sounds of the two, and then we made "Pencil Lead Music" by doodling with both pencils at once. It was fantastic, and something I could have easily missed out on if I'd been rigidly focused on simply getting the worksheet finished.

Having a child is like getting a gift that continues to unwrap itself. As our kids grow and become more themselves, we're allowed—*if we pay attention*—to continue to be dazzled by a new quality or characteristic that heretofore has been unseen. But many of us are so distracted as we navigate the various "tasks" of parenting that we miss the moments of really connecting with our kids. It is those moments that allow us to truly see who they are and who they're becoming. When the time and conversations we have with our children are focused around getting them to take their vitamins, rinse their dinner dishes, or take their baths, we're skimming the surface of the adventure of parenting. It's like traveling to Hawaii and staying in the hotel room to watch movies.

The most poignant confessions some of my clients have made to me have been their realization that they had been so minimally present as they were raising their children that when the kids finally left the nest, they looked back on those eighteen years with no idea where they had gone. More importantly, many parents find themselves looking at their eighteen-year-olds and realizing they don't really know them.

The finest "university" one can attend is a funeral. When we listen to someone being memorialized by those who loved and cared about him, the concerns that so often distract us in our daily lives are put into perspective. Invariably, it's the moments of sweetness and joy that were tucked in between one's daily achievements that truly matter.

Life is ultimately a string of moments gathered into hours, days, weeks, months, and years. If in a quiet moment we ask ourselves what we really want for our children, and our answer has something to do with them being truly content throughout their lives, then one of the most important gifts we can offer them is the ability to be present so they can experience all the joy and richness available to them. The sense of peace and fulfillment that comes from quietly and genuinely appreciating each day may not come with a flashing neon sign, but it is our best bet that we're going to end up with a life full of deeply, fully, and passionately lived moments.

Games to play with your child that encourage being present and mindful

- **Bear Belly Breathing:** Have the child lie on her back with a small stuffed animal on her belly. As she breathes, she watches her belly rise up and down. Helps children to focus and relax.
- **Pinwheel:** With nice, slow breaths keep the belly soft while blowing pinwheel.
- **Tingly hands:** Rub your hands together quickly for a few seconds, and then notice the warmth and tingly feelings. Allow those sensations to bring you back to your body and to the present moment.
- **Straw breathing:** Breathe in normally, then breathe out very gently through a straw. Put the hand that isn't holding the straw at the end of the straw to make sure you don't feel a gust of air; the exhale should be so gentle that you don't feel air coming out. When most of the air has been released, remove the straw from your mouth and finish exhaling normally. After one or two breaths, resume the exercise.
- **Shake and dance:** Soft belly breathing as you stand up and shake, shake, shake to the beat of a drum. Then stop and balance in an interesting position.
- **Chocolate:** Open chocolate as if you're in slow motion. Listen to the paper crinkling. Put the chocolate in your mouth and move it around with your tongue, noticing what it tastes like without chewing or swallowing. Allow it to melt. Notice what you're experiencing while you're experiencing it without labeling it good or bad.

- **Walking:** Notice what it feels like to walk in socks, just feeling each part of your foot as it makes contact with the floor.

Questions and Suggestions

Question: *Being mindful and present* sounds *good, but the truth is, I'm busy from morning to night. I have a job, a demanding husband, a house to take care of, four children, and two dogs. It doesn't seem realistic to think about dropping everything to gaze into my son or daughter's eyes every time they need something from me. Do you have any other suggestions for incorporating these ideas into a busy life?*

Suggestion: I understand. Far be it from me to suggest you cut the phone line or stop the clocks. With everything you have on your plate, I wouldn't expect you to be able to drift from room to room, soulfully connecting with each family member (and dog) while dinner burns and the baby's diaper needs changing. Being mindful doesn't require us to get a lobotomy. While gazing for hours at the endless panorama of the Serengeti offered me a terrific chance to practice truly slowing down, bringing stillness into our day-to-day lives doesn't require us to make dramatic changes in our lifestyle. In fact, I would venture to say that there are many people who, by outward appearance, live in a very off-the-grid way but still miss out on being fully present from moment to moment.

The shifts that need to happen to become more present are much more internal than they are external, although I strongly believe many of us over schedule our children and ourselves. Regardless of how long your to-do list is or how many different things are pulling on you, all you're ever doing is what you're doing in this very moment. If you can step into that mindset, noticing the tingling in your fingers and the sensation of aliveness in your chest while you change the baby's diaper and quiz your seven-year-old on his spelling words, you'll discover that it's not so much about how quiet or chaotic life appears on the outside but rather how much awareness—and even reverence—we bring to the tasks we're engaged in.

Take small steps, bite-sized attempts to simply be more conscious in this moment, and you will have started to live—and teach your children—in a way that lets you receive more enjoyment out of each interaction and experience as you move through your day. If you forget, just pick up in the next moment and start again.

***

Question: *In today's world, multitasking is the order of the day. What you're suggesting might be good for children who are going to grow up and live on a farm or something, but I want my son and daughters to be prepared for life in the real world, and that involves moving pretty fast through the day. Isn't it good to be able to do many things at once?*

Suggestion: I agree that the pace of the lives that most of us find ourselves living moves quite a bit faster than it did years ago or still does in rural environments and small towns. I don't have a problem with teaching children ways to plan and organize so they're able to accomplish tasks appropriate to the world in which they live. (That doesn't mean, however, that I think the pace we move at is right or in synch with our wiring; I still maintain that we're over stimulating our children—and ourselves—by trying to cram too much into every hour of every day.) But I do think we can agree that the *quality* of the tasks we take on is what matters most, since this is what allows us to feel a sense of satisfaction about how we've spent the irreplaceable moments of our day.

The shifts I'm proposing don't require you to restructure your life. If you believe Susie needs to do ballet *and* tutoring Monday through Thursday, and soccer on Fridays and Saturdays, *and she's enjoying it*, then go for it. Just make sure these activities aren't robbing your children—or you—of joy.

When you're driving your children to their various activities, are you tense or are you having a good time? Do you curse at the red light and honk at the driver who took "your" parking place, or do your children experience humor and fun in the midst of the whirlwind of everyone's activities? When you're sitting together at dinner (which I hope you do most nights), do you taste the food, savoring and chewing it, or are you throwing it down your throat as you run around the house looking for your cell phone charger? At unexpected moments do you catch yourself inhaling and being grateful and awed by the breath coming in and out on its own, or are you oblivious to the invisible miracles around you?

One of the things I so love about children is their perceptiveness and honesty. Simply doing nothing isn't the same as being present; if you're busy and active but taking time to smell the roses, your children will learn how to live in the moment *and* get things done. It's not an either/or proposition. What matters most is pausing now and again to savor life as it's unfolding in the moment in front of you. If your kids see you doing that, and they watch you *enjoying* the many things you're juggling, they'll learn how to live more mindfully.

***

Question: *I'd like to be more present and in the moment, but the truth is, I'm pretty hyperactive and restless. I pride myself on my ability to do several things at once, but what I'm realizing is that I'm not very good at doing just one thing at a time. Do you have any advice for how I can ease myself into a mindful way of living without going nuts?*

Suggestion: As a fellow hyper-human, I completely relate to this question. There once was a time when I believed that to be mentally quiet I needed to be physically still as well. I do believe there's value in bringing body and mind to a screeching halt and settling quietly into the moment; if I'm having a beautiful experience within, my body does eventually settle down into a very deep peace. But I've also come to see that the sweetness inherent in any given moment is by no means picky about whether we're in motion or stationary.

Move! Dance! Climb a tree or wiggle your feet. Just be in a state of awareness as you do what you do. Those who practice mindfulness have written much on the subject of walking meditations, and you might enjoy reading some of that material. Meanwhile, I would encourage you to be who you are.

Shift your attention more and more to noticing what your foot feels like as it hits the pavement, or how the water feels as you're washing your hands, and you'll have started living more fully in the now. As you practice this, it may happen that you'll become more comfortable with breathing exercises that have a quieting effect on the nervous system, which might help you feel less restless in your skin. However it happens, taste, smell, feel, and live in a state of alertness and reverence, and you'll savor far more   of   the   precious   moments   of   life.

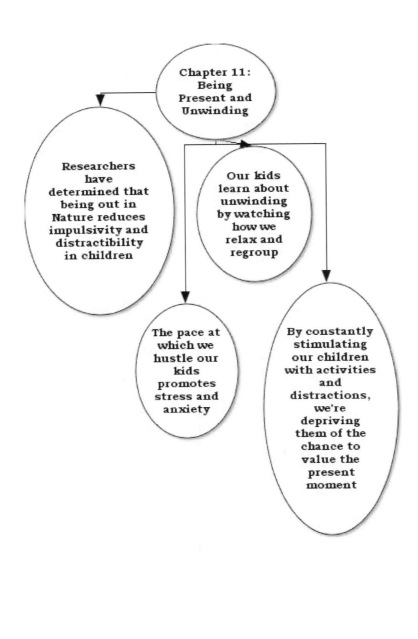

Chapter 11: Being Present and Unwinding

Researchers have determined that being out in Nature reduces impulsivity and distractibility in children

Our kids learn about unwinding by watching how we relax and regroup

The pace at which we hustle our kids promotes stress and anxiety

By constantly stimulating our children with activities and distractions, we're depriving them of the chance to value the present moment

Chapter Twelve
Launching Children Towards a Life of True Happiness

"Happiness lies within you, and thus it is your treasure."
Prem Rawat

One of the benefits of having a counseling practice in Malibu, California, is the chance to unequivocally understand that money, fame, and power are unrelated to a person's true joy. Our culture collectively pushes the idea that there's an extra dose of happiness available to those who achieve notable fame or fortune, which leaves the rest of us either pushing relentlessly to get ahead so we can finally "get there", or feeling resigned to living without deep satisfaction. I've worked with some of the most famous, wealthy, and powerful people in the world; when they come into my office and open their hearts, their longing for contentment is identical to that of every other person I've ever known.

Loneliness, depression, and discontent are unrelated to how many houses we own or how expensive our sunglasses are. All humans come with a built-in thirst for true peace, real love and a sense of being homesick that nags at the heart, following us around as we move through our day with a sense of unrest and dissatisfaction, even after we've gotten the longed-for toy, job, or spouse.

The call from within is a gift, if recognized as such; we are meant to be nourished from the well of our hearts, where authentic joy and contentment reign supreme. Parents give themselves—and their children—a magnificent gift when they demonstrate the importance of honoring the still, small voice that invites us to partake of the riches within, rather than ignoring that inner thirst. *Parenting Without Power Struggles* is about helping preserve our children's natural-born joy and enjoyment of life. But beyond that, it's about inspiring our children to live their very best lives; and that includes understanding that the ultimate source of happiness is and always will be within themselves.

We live in extraordinary times. One could say that the darkness has never been darker, but then again, the light is shining very brightly as well. Millions of people logged onto the Internet to listen to Eckhart Tolle and Oprah Winfrey conduct a teleclass about living in the moment. Movies and books like *The Secret* are transforming the way people think about their day-to-day lives— ordinary people, not just old hippies or diehard New Agers. Marianne Williamson has a daily radio show teaching *A Course in Miracles*. Prem Rawat[1] has presented his message about inner peace to over ten million people worldwide. It is indeed a time of unprecedented interest in stepping beyond the confines of old ways of thinking that suggested a successful life consisted merely in getting a good education, having a marriage that held together, and kids who managed to do more or less the same.

At the same time, our youngsters are being raised in rather strange times, exposed to an unprecedented level of superficiality and empty promises on television, the Internet, and even their cell phones. There's an alarming potential for loneliness and isolation in the midst of all this noise. Without a sense of rootedness that comes from within, the allure of numbing out via drugs, promiscuity, and workaholism becomes dangerously real.

It's wonderful to raise our children to feel cherished and seen by us, celebrated for their unique gifts and empowered to envision and create their best lives. But if we can encourage them—in word and deed—to honor the relentless calling of their hearts, we give them what matters most: the ability to feel peace and contentment regardless of external circumstances.

There is a hidden treasure within each of us that's portable and available if we pay attention to it, even in the midst of the storms of life. When we don't have access to that inner sanctum of peace and joy, we move through our lives rudderless. There's a restlessness among young adults, an impatience for things to finally happen, for something big to come together and bring contentment and happiness.

This is the age-old illusion, or what I call the Big Fat Lie. Until we realize that what we are looking for is within, we'll continue to run the rat race, pretending to our kids that satisfaction is just around the corner, meanwhile keeping ourselves—and them—on that old hamster wheel, never arriving where we truly need to be.

Whatever your religious beliefs or spiritual leanings, I encourage you to remember the importance of offering your children the awareness that, as Antoine de Exupéry stated so simply in *The Little Prince*², "What is essential is invisible to the eye." We carry within us a portable paradise, a literal factory of joy that follows us wherever we are, in good times and in bad. By paying attention to the little spark of gratitude or sweetness that tickles your heart, you'll help it grow, just as a plant blossoms when it's given water and sunlight. Rather than being fooled into believing that happiness is just around the corner or is only available if you achieve or acquire something, allow yourself to bathe in the gifts scattered at your feet. When your children see *you* living this way, they will understand that, as beneficial as it is to envision having successful lives, they can enjoy the truest fulfillment right now by discovering it at its source—within their hearts.

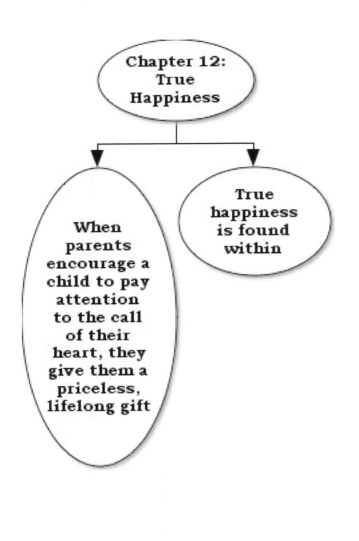

Chapter Thirteen
Empowering Kids to Create Their Very Best Lives

"Parents can only give good advice or put them on the right paths, but the final forming of a person's character lies in their own hands."
Anne Frank

Successful adults generally have the sense that they arrived where they are through intention, commitment, and effort rather than simply as a result of random events. They feel not only a sense of pleasure in their achievements—whether those are material, relational, emotional, or circumstantial—but also the satisfaction of having overcome whatever obstacles might have otherwise prevented their accomplishment. Adults who see themselves as being in the driver's seat of their lives feel a general sense of pride, not only in their specific achievements but also in their ability to create their lives. They know they could apply the same skills and intentions that got them where they are to any number of other goals and they would experience the same measure of success. They feel empowered to make their dreams come true.

While it's wonderful for kids to have parents who encourage them, many children who have had supportive and loving parents nonetheless become adults who cannot seem to overcome the roadblocks that prevent them from achieving their life goals. Empowering kids to create the life best suited to who they are requires more than positive thinking, belief in luck, or parents who consistently tell them, "You can do anything." And while a formal education certainly offers a child advantages, we cannot help but notice that millions of well-educated adults cannot claim to have realized their hopes and dreams. In addition, there are countless stories of children who grew up in the midst of tremendous hardship—without supportive parents or a good education—who managed to create very satisfying adult lives. Clearly, having parents who cheer them on or earning a college degree isn't a guarantee that a child will enjoy a successful adulthood.

What, then, are the abilities or skills that best predict whether a child will be equipped to live his very best life? I believe there are five qualities that help youngsters move towards adult life with the resources needed to find their passion, manage the obstacles that may get in their way, and persevere towards making their dreams come true. These five qualities are *resilience, self-respect, problem solving, visioning,* and *gratitude.*

> There are five qualities or abilities that help a youngster move towards adult life with the resources needed to find their passion, manage the obstacles that may get in their way, and persevere towards making their dreams come true: *resilience, self-respect, problem-solving, visioning* and *gratitude.*

Resilience

Nature provides children with endless opportunities to become resilient human beings. As tempting as it is to buffer our kids from the bumps in the road as they grow up, it's knowing they can hit a bump and still continue on that fortifies our children to become adults who are able to withstand setbacks and challenges and get where they want to go in their lives.

When children grow up knowing they can live through sadness and frustration, they become capable of tremendous resourcefulness and resolve. If they develop the ability to be flexible, they feel confident to try another approach when this one isn't working. By learning to question negative thinking that might promote someone else to give up, they are liberated from the beliefs that lead to defeat or hopelessness.

If parents help their children feel their feelings fully, while guiding them towards the confidence that comes from knowing they can cope with life's ups and downs, their children head towards adulthood capable of hanging in there when the going gets tough, or letting go when it's time to move on. Resilient children become resilient adults, far better prepared to engage courageously and passionately with life.

Self-respect

As much as parents have come to believe their praise is instrumental in helping foster their children's positive sense of self, true self-esteem is not built by fussing over children's accomplishments. Kids know their parents are biased about their achievements. They hunger for honest feedback about what they've accomplished.

Authentic self-respect is built on the deep understanding that you matter. This isn't something parents can simply hand over to their kids; it's developed when children have opportunities to interact with the real world and offer something of themselves to others. This helps them come to the practical understanding that their efforts have actually improved someone else's life. It's a heady feeling to look someone in the eye and receive his thanks for handing him a meal; or to watch a young child begin to learn to read because you sat beside her, helping her sound out words; or to see a proud new pet owner walk away with an orphaned dog that you helped match him with at a pet adoption fair. By the time children are six or seven, I urge parents to give their children the chance to help others in some small way that gives them the sense of meaning that comes from being useful.

Volunteering and mentoring are potent ways of helping kids develop a positive sense of self-respect. But I also encourage parents to make sure their children contribute to keeping their home functional and clean. I'm a great believer in chores, and I think that kids from the age of three or so deserve the satisfaction that comes from taking responsibility for some aspect of maintaining the day-to-day workings at home. When my son was little, I let him sweep and help with the laundry. Now, at eighteen, he has two hours of chores each weekend doing things around the house like repairing the fence, fertilizing plants, or washing windows.

By knowing they're capable of contributing to their personal care (making their beds, brushing their teeth) as well as helping things run smoothly in their family's lives, kids develop a sense of independence and self-reliance that help them become competent adults. When youngsters discover that their time and effort can uplift the life of someone else, they not only feel a deep sense of value but also have the opportunity to develop a more authentic appreciation for what they have.

I've worked with wealthy individuals, parents who can and do provide everything materially imaginable for their kids but who nonetheless exhibit an insatiable hunger for more *stuff*, or who suffer from an ongoing sense of emptiness and sadness. I've also worked with immensely well-to-do people who understood the benefits to their children of earning their own money for special items, helping others, or living in moderation. True self-esteem cannot be bought; rather, it comes from discovering what we really *are* capable of doing, and it is an essential element in launching a child towards a successful adulthood. (There's a great little movie I recommend about today's culture of acquisition at *www.storyofstuff.com.*)

The ability to solve problems

Eckhart Tolle[1] suggests that problems exist only in the context of the future or the past. If you ask someone in the midst of a divorce or facing a job layoff how they're doing, the only way they can truly be suffering from their problem is if they're projecting it into their future or bringing it up from their past. In the moment, how they're doing is okay—sitting and having a conversation with you, drinking tea, or watering the roses. Thought of in this way, there actually are no problems.

Lest this come across as too metaphysical or heartless, Tolle goes on to say that there are certainly circumstances where someone could be struggling with something in this moment, like dealing with a splinter in her finger or a colicky newborn who won't stop crying. But he redefines those as *challenges* rather than problems. It's interesting how a simple shift in outlook and semantics has the potential to impact our perceptions and, consequently, how we feel about our circumstances.

I like this way of thinking. When we worry about the future, we feed fear. If our kids could learn to resist the temptation to project potential problems into the future or dwell on old troubles from the past, they would be far better equipped to deal effectively with challenges in the present.

That said, I also believe a successful adult is someone who has learned to solve problems creatively. One of my favorite approaches is mind mapping, which I usually do on paper but which can also be done on the computer. (My favorite program for this is available at *www.inspiration.com.*) Kids are naturals at brainstorming creative solutions when they're stuck. I teach them to write a short description of the challenge (not problem) in the center of a page and then create branches moving outward, each with a possible solution. The next step involves creating subheadings listing the resources (time, money, people) required for each potential solution. The following figure is an example of a problem-solving mind map I did with Jenna, who wanted to bring up her algebra grade and could only come up with one or two options for doing so.

Another approach is to list the pros and cons of each choice, as shown in the following diagram I created to help a youngster decide whether or not to try out for the swim team.

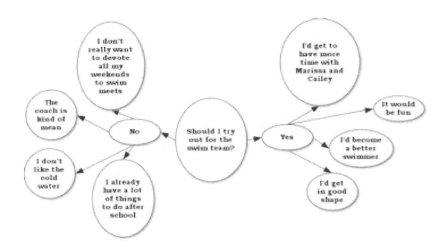

Ask the future you

Sometimes, when my son is faced with a difficult decision, I encourage him to ask the future version of himself what *he* would recommend. In other words, I suggest he imagine himself five or ten years down the road and have a conversation with that older, hopefully wiser self to see what *he* would advise. Another idea I've shared is the Deathbed Test. I invite my son to imagine himself at the very end of his life, and to ask *that* Ari how to solve the predicament he's facing *today*. These techniques can help youngsters put their dilemmas in a larger context, avoid making impulsive choices, and see challenging situations from a more mature perspective. Children who have a repertoire of creative approaches to dealing with life's challenges—without transforming them into problems by projecting them into the future—feel confident about their ability to come up with solutions to situations which might otherwise feel daunting.

Visioning

Another way we help empower kids to live their best lives is to teach them how to envision the manifestations of their passions and goals. I'm a big fan of the book *The Passion Test*, which introduces a very simple, usable way of helping uncover one's five most meaningful goals. I also love Martha Beck's *Finding Your Own North Star* (I maintain an updated list of related books on my website, *www.passionateparenting.net*). As our kids get older, we give them a tremendous gift when we encourage them to explore the things that help them feel joyful and alive so they can picture—and make real—their ideal lives. For most children and teens, their interests may change, and that's as it should be. Kids need to know that life is indeed like a buffet and it's fine to try different interests as they grow up.

Regardless of what today's dream may be, it's wonderful if we can teach our children some of what have come to be called the Laws of Attraction. In simpler terms (and before *The Secret* was written) this means focusing on any and all evidence and support that is in the service of our dreams coming true. The Laws of Attraction suggest that we get more of what we focus on; they offer a way to feel more in the driver's seat as we participate in creating the lives we're best suited to live. This includes having faith that the universe is indeed benevolent and that we are supported in ways we might not rationally understand but that are at work nonetheless. As Marianne Williamson[2] so eloquently says, "Faith isn't blind. It's visionary."

Some kids love to make vision boards, where they clip pictures from magazines and create a collage of images that help them see themselves living their ideal lives. For someone whose dream is to go a particular university, his vision board might include scenes of student life at that university, logos, headlines from the school's student newspaper, and so on. For a youngster whose dream is to dance with the American Ballet Theater, her vision board might include images of past and current dancers, various performances, and so on.

Another interesting way of empowering a child to bring his dreams to reality is to show him how to create a YouTube Vision Statement. The youngster weaves symbolic words, phrases, and images into movie form, along with appropriately inspiring music, and posts it on YouTube or a similar site—

effectively announcing his dreams to the world, and watching it frequently to reinforce the emotions of having that experience.

For kids who don't have a sense yet of their passion or interests, I urge parents to take a look at Howard Gardner and Thomas Armstrong's work with Multiple Intelligence. By doing some simple exercises, readers can gain great clarity towards staying on track with their natural passions.

Regardless of their specific dreams and goals, all children should be encouraged to envision a life where they feel happy, healthy, and connected to those they care about.

Gratitude

The last element in this list of qualities that contribute to a child becoming a successful adult is gratitude. Although many would claim that this isn't really a skill as much as a state of mind, I believe that as parents we can cultivate a child's natural sense of appreciation—or not. The most powerful way we "teach" gratitude is, of course, by living with appreciation ourselves on a day-to-day basis. Children gather their lessons best from observing how the important adults in their world conduct themselves. If our kids see us chronically complaining or arguing, they absorb that way of approaching life.

However, when we demonstrate a cheerfulness and thankfulness about the gifts that come our way—large and small—our children learn that there is always something to appreciate. This "Attitude of Gratitude" creates a mindset that is more receptive to noticing—and magnifying—the events and moments of our days that are in the service of our dreams. In other words, by paying attention to even the most seemingly inconsequential evidence that things are going in a direction that's in synch with our goals, we position ourselves to receive more of the same.

I like a little book by Michael Losier called *Law of Attraction*. Some people understand the value of envisioning what they want, but they don't really *know* what they want. A useful activity from Losier's book is to list what you *don't* want, and then turn that into a list of what you *do* want. If your youngster says, "I don't want to hang out with the kids who tease other kids all the time," you'd help her say, "Then you *do* want to hang out with kids who are kind to other kids." He suggests avoiding the words "don't," "not," and "no."

Another helpful component is bragging about any and all evidence that what you want is coming your way. Incorporate into your child's day the chance to tell you—or perhaps the whole family, around the dinner table—five things she feels grateful for that point to her dreams coming ever closer. If one of your daughter's dreams is to become a singer, she might share the fact that she learned all the words to a song she liked a lot from a movie she just saw. Some kids like to write daily in a gratitude journal. Others like to share what they're grateful for as they climb into bed at the end of the day.

Many children feel a chronic sense of powerlessness as they move through their day-to-day lives. For the most part, their time is spent doing what they're told, whether they feel like it or not. They have to go to school, obey other people's rules, be quiet when they feel like talking, and do homework they generally dislike. They're told what they can eat, when they can socialize, and with whom.

There's a sense of vitality and freedom that comes when kids get to shift from being victims of their circumstances to recognizing the multitude of ways they can manifest the lives they are uniquely designed to live. As parents, we need to vitalize the understanding that we can each be in the driver's seat of our lives, breaking through limitations and exuberantly designing the lives we're meant to live with confidence, joy, and passion.

Questions and Suggestions

Question: *I like the idea of helping my son and daughter feel empowered to create their most suitable lives, but I don't want them to get their hopes up. What happens if they use these techniques and they still have to have a job flipping burgers at McDonald's to help them get through college?*

Suggestion: I would hope that your son and daughter will have enough opportunities to develop resilience in their younger years that they will be okay with flipping burgers at McDonald's while they are in college. In fact, for many kids, having a job that's not right up their alley is an important rite of passage. But let's do hope they get their hopes up—and keep them up!—about feeling empowered to live their best lives. It seems to me that our mindset can be a great predictor of what we believe to be possible or impossible.

Reverend Michael Beckwith recently told the story of a renowned mathematician who, as a college student, had unknowingly worked out two previously unsolvable math problems. Even Einstein had been unable to solve them. The student had misunderstood his math professor and believed the solution to the two problems were due the following week. Even though they were immensely challenging, he thought to himself, "Someone's going to work them out. Why not me?" His professor was flabbergasted. The operative element was simply his ignorance of the limitations that prevented his fellow students from pursuing the solutions.

As long as you are also helping your kids develop resilience, I would encourage your children to get their hopes very much up as they think about the lives they want to live. With hope come optimism, confidence, and the willingness to break through obstacles to make our dreams come true.

***

Question: *I work very hard at my job and have done so for the last seventeen years, largely so I can provide my wife and kids with a comfortable life that allows them to mostly have what they want. Are you saying I shouldn't give my children what I'm able to, just so they can build character?*

Suggestion: Yes, sort of. I commend you for working hard to provide a comfortable life for your family, and I understand that it can feel wonderful to be able to buy whatever your kids ask for. But experience tells me that in the long run, parents do their children a disservice when they operate like a cash machine, providing whatever is on their children's wish lists in an attempt to make them happy.

Children learn delayed gratification by dealing with frustration and disappointment when they don't get what they want right away. In addition, material possessions often take on a much greater value for children when they've had to save up and pay for things out of their own *earned* money.

You may not agree, and of course you need to do what feels right to you. But in my opinion, no matter how much money you earn, it's important that children be allowed to long for things, to feel their disappointed when their wishes aren't granted right away, and to discover the difference between what they *want* and what they *need*.

This was never clearer to me than when I took my son to Africa. The big-ticket item for children there was a writing pen, which most families could not afford. We brought a big box of pens to give away, and when a child received one, you would have thought she'd just been given a brand-new computer or a fancy outfit. What was most touching was that when we ran out of pens, the empty-handed children were just as gracious and sweet as the ones who had received one. It put a lot into perspective. I would encourage you to give your children more of what they need most from you—love, connection, time, and support—and less of the things that only money can buy.

***

Question: *I think teaching a child mind mapping to problem-solve sounds interesting, but my son is only eight and fortunately, his life is pretty good. Is there a way to introduce this technique to him if he doesn't have any problems? ?*

Suggestion: Absolutely! Young children love mind maps, and learn very quickly how to work use them not only for solving problems, but also for making decisions, planning a birthday party or organizing a book report.

Have fun with mind maps! Give your son an extra large pad of newsprint and let him start with mapping the ways he might save up for a new bike. Encourage him to mind map the pros and cons of signing up to be a cafeteria helper. Or help him make a mind map to help him choose what to read for his next book report.

While mind mapping is done just fine on paper, there is a great program for the computer that has some great features, including the ability to create outlines from mind map diagrams with a single keystroke. The company that makes Inspiration also makes a version called Kidspiration for younger kids that is a wonderful tool for helping children generate creative writing ideas.

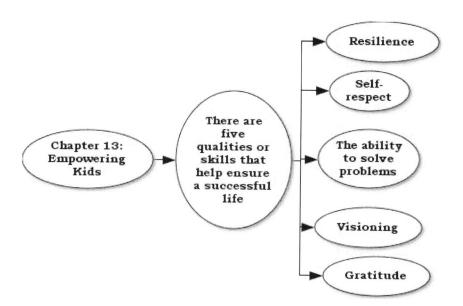

Chapter Fourteen
Live Like Your Kids Are Watching—Because They Are

This afternoon, as I waited outside my son's school to give him a ride home, I watched a young man laughing with friends. He was extremely tall and lanky--and looked vaguely familiar--but from a distance he was unrecognizable. As I watched him a little longer, my heart split open with a tender love; that six-foot-five young man was my son! How could that be? But there he was, and despite many protestations on my part (internally), he is racing towards the day when he will be off on the adventure of his own life, an adventure I won't be able to watch from twenty feet away, as I am today.

Last night I wandered into Ari's room. He invited me to hear the lineup for an upcoming weekend concert he plans to go to. I settled myself on the end of his bed and listened to him recite a long list of band names for the three days of the concert. I recognized roughly one out of about twenty (ugh). Afterwards, he feverishly texted friends about who was going to be playing, smiling to himself as he read or delivered a comment. I sat there feeling as though I had landed in heaven, soaking him in with the heightened awareness that comes from realizing that, indeed, moments like these will not go on forever.

My son is approaching his adulthood. And something in me is undeniably aware that this window of opportunity for me to give him whatever I can on a daily, hourly basis is changing. While I realize that I will always be his Momma and hopefully available to him for love and support for decades to come, this chance to be with him day to day and influence him in the thousands of ways I do—consciously *and* unconsciously—will come to an end. So I do my best to pay attention, be conscious, and get it as right as I can.

As our children grow older and manifest more of who they are, we get to see how we have shaped them. While many of us do our best to offer our wisdom and counsel when our kids hit a bump or cross a line, most of us are unaware that the majority of what we pass on to them happens as they observe how we live and what we stand for in the ordinary moments of our lives. As Ari edges ever closer to the point where he *won't* be living here with me, I become acutely aware of the ways I have influenced who he is by how he has watched me conduct my life.

It's easy to forget this when our children are little. We enter a stage of timelessness when a baby arrives. It's impossible to comprehend that a day will come when our kids won't be under our roof, needing a ride or a sandwich. We're swept into the whirlwind, becoming so immersed in the endless tasks and demands of being a parent that we don't realize how intensely our children are observing us.

Once in a while the voyeur in me tunes in to one of the reality TV shows. I've always wondered why people would do or say the things they do when they know the cameras are rolling. There she is, arguing with her friend and spewing the most ridiculous commentary—the kinds of remarks that she'll later regret saying to her friend, let alone the rest of the world! I could never understand how people could behave as they do when they know they are being filmed, until one day it hit me: It's because the cameras are *always* rolling, 24/7. Eventually, the camera recedes into the background and the participants in the reality shows are oblivious to its presence.

The same is true for us as parents. The camera is always rolling. Our children are always watching. They watch us thank a stranger for holding a door open for us. They watch us grip the steering wheel, cursing at the red light. They watch us drop money into the Salvation Army bucket. They watch us gossip to one friend about how boring another friend is. They watch us when we express our loving care to an aging aunt. They watch us when we complain about how fat we are or how impossible it is to lose weight. They watch when we make arrangements for dinner deliveries to a neighbor who isn't feeling well. They watch when we blame our spouse, or our boss, or them, when things aren't going right in our world. They watch when we make mistakes and apologize, and they watch when we don't. The cameras are rolling 24/7; our kids are *constantly* watching, whether we are aware of it or not.

When our children are demanding toddlers or surly teenagers, we may long for the day when they finally move out and move on, liberating us from the challenges and demands of raising them. We all have those days. But hopefully, if we're having a generally good time on this ride of raising our kids, we're mostly enjoying the feeling that this arrangement—splashy baths, fascinating conversations, messy tears, thrown-together meals, epic Monopoly games, fluorescent Band-Aids, impossible science projects, sloppy kisses—is forever. The thing is, it isn't. Those 24/7 cameras eventually pack up and leave the house, the cameraman disappears and goes home, and our children march off into the horizon, launched into lives where we are supporting cast members, occasional visitors.

The lessons we want to pass on to our children about living with joy, resilience, and authenticity are taught by living them in front of our kids, day in and day out. When they see us taking a class in something we've always been interested in, volunteering at a shelter, or sitting calmly at a traffic light, our children are offered a Technicolor vision of what life looks like when it's lived with passion, appreciation, and adaptation. If we want our kids to be less defensive and more receptive to our input, we need to show them what that looks like. If our kids give us what my son calls "honest feedback," we might want to consider whether they're telling us something about ourselves that might be true. When Ari tells me he thinks I use too much salt, I tell him I think he's right. If I say something in front of guests that he later says was embarrassing, I respond by saying he's got a point and I'll consider his view about it.

When someone criticizes us, it gets very interesting when we don't resist or defend, and instead tell them we can see why she'd see it that way, or even say, "You could be right!" By living this way in front of our children, we show them that Being Right isn't the Holy Grail after all, and that if we're open and not resistant, we may get some great insights from others.

As much as we like to lecture and advise our children, the true lessons we teach our kids are embedded in our actions. So, remember, the cameras are rolling. Make sure the majority of what your kids see on that film isn't what you'll later wish could end up cut and piled on the editing floor. We need to be as conscious as we can as we parent. When we make mistakes, the thing to do is to apologize sincerely, and not justify or blame someone else for *making* us do whatever it is we're apologizing for. Say you're sorry, with a BIG, FAT PERIOD. Use good manners. Speak kindly.

Here's what it boils down to, for me. If we sign up for the full parenting package, the *Parenting Without Power Struggles* package, we aren't just helping our children grow up. We get to grow up, too. That means we continue setting the intention to live in a way that shows our children what it looks like to keep growing, and to keep growing up. It's the ride of a lifetime, full of surprises, challenges, and extraordinary opportunities to become the best version of ourselves that we can be—while our kids are watching.

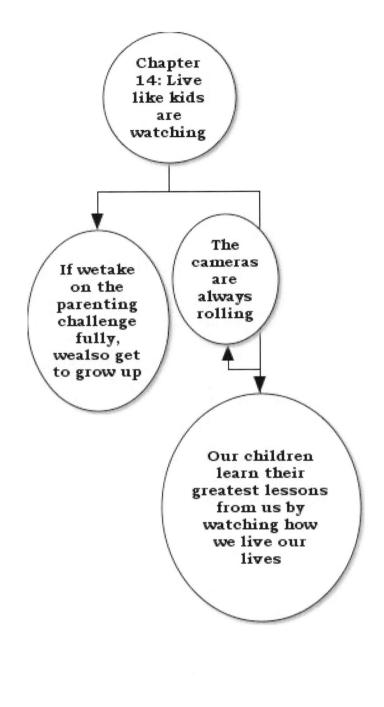

Susan and son, Ari

"Where Do I Go from Here?"

Now for the fun part: the opportunity to take an honest look at how you're doing, and the chance to set goals and intentions towards improving day-to-day life as you raise your children.

The checklists that follow are included for one and only one purpose, and that is to help you get an objective sense of how your parenting life is going, and the opportunity to track it by repeating the checklists regularly. (Additional copies are available at the link for *Parenting Without Power Struggles* bonus material at the end of the book.)

These checklists are *not* intended to discourage you. We all—myself included—sometimes fall prey to frustration, fatigue, and old habits; the first checklist can be humbling. But it can also be a useful tool to help us discover the specific things we want to work on. At the end of this section you'll have a chance to choose which goals you want to work on first and the opportunity to set clear intentions about how you'd like things between you and your child to improve.

Use these assessments as reminders to apply the techniques you've learned in this book to release the upsetting triggers that promote stress and anger that sometimes causes you to lose your cool. Apply the results to help you decide which ways you want to nourish the connection you have with your children. Take forward what you learn about helping your children when they're frustrated or when they tempt you to engage in power struggles and negotiations. Let the results of the checklists help you remember to listen and translate your children's feelings rather than rush to apply logic in an attempt to get them to feel better.

I advise you to remember how vital it is that you keep in mind the importance of taking care of *yourself* physically and emotionally, maintaining a viable network of support to help you parent, making sure your life provides you with opportunities to nourish your own spirit as you take care of those around you.

I encourage you to use the "Intentions" section at the end of this chapter to help you determine where you want to go from here. Make your intentions clear, observable, *and positive.*

Instead of writing, "I want to stop nagging my kids so much," say, "I want to speak kindly, and use the *Request into the Yes* approach." Rather than saying, "I don't want to bark orders at my children," say, "I want to use humor when I talk to my kids."

Please, PLEASE, use this checklist in a positive way. You get to be a *tired* mother, an *impatient* father, or a *cranky* parent, but saying "I'm a terrible parent" is no longer allowed! Neither is "I did it wrong!" or "I blew it" There *is* no right or wrong. Guilt and shame have no place in the *Parenting Without Power Struggles* world. Let go of those negative ways of evaluating yourself.

Then start noticing when you do something—anything—in service of one of your positive intentions. If you stop yourself right before you shout at your kids, make a mental note, or better yet, log it in a *Parenting Without Power Struggles* journal. If you use the Four Questions to untangle yourself from an upset, acknowledge it and give yourself a round of applause.

As parents, we have the most demanding challenge on earth. We will inevitably trip and fall. The trick isn't to become a robotic Stepford parent; it's to embrace our humanity, show ourselves kindness when we stumble, and keep on keepin' on.

If we want our children to respect and appreciate us, we're going to have to show them what that looks like by treating ourselves with respect and appreciation.

Best of luck, and stay in touch by visiting *www.parentingwithoutpowerstruggles.com*, where I will continue to add new tips, ideas and information.

Parenting Without Power Struggles Checklist #1

A reminder to live like your kids are watching . . . because they are.

For additional copies visit
http://www.parentingwithoutpowerstruggles.com

Answer honestly: **0** = Never   **1** = Occasionally   **2** = Frequently   **3** = Most of the time

(For a more positive version, please skip Checklist #1 and move on to Checklist #2)

____ 1. I often feel my children are running the show, or that I'm negotiating for the job of being the one in charge.

____ 2. I lose my cool, telling my children it's their fault I'm out of control, doing and saying things that I later regret.

____ 3. I find it hard to spend one-on-one time with my children, or to make it a priority.

____ 4. I exhibit stressful behaviors (clenching the steering wheel, muttering negative comments) when I'm at a stoplight, placed on hold, or stuck in some kind of line.

____ 5. I cave in when my children are frustrated, and give them what they want to avoid their upset or badgering.

____ 6. I threaten, bribe, or shout at my spouse/children/parents or give them the cold shoulder when I'm upset with them.

____ 7. When I'm not doing anything, I turn on my computer, make a phone call, or start watching TV or a movie so I won't feel bored.

____ 8. I use logic to try to talk my children out of their upsetting feelings and beliefs.

____ 9. I defend myself and blame others when things go wrong, whether I'm guilty or not.

____ 10. My children observe me using tobacco, alcohol, or other medications to feel better or when I need to relax.

____ 11. My children observe me worrying a lot and expressing anxiety on a regular basis about what *might* happen or might go wrong.

_____ 12. I interrupt my children when they're telling me something, or I prepare my rebuttal while they're speaking.

_____ 13. My children observe me saying, "Yes" to people's requests and then griping about what I agreed to do.

_____ 14. I tend to live in the past or the future rather than in the present moment.

_____ 15. I speak negatively about other people behind their backs in front of my children.

_____ 16. I admonish my children to improve, change, or somehow be different from who they are.

Scoring

0- 16: Keep up the good work!

17- 30: You may want to set the goal of working on one challenging area each week as you commit to making some positive shifts.

30-48 Please consider finding support for your efforts to improve things in your parenting life. I encourage you to sign up for the *Parenting Without Power Struggles* newsletter or teleclasses for ongoing support.

Parenting Without Power Struggles Checklist #2

For additional copies visit
http://www.parentingwithoutpowerstruggles.com

0 = Never   **1** = Occasionally   **2** = Frequently   **3** = Most of the time

___ 1. My children know that I'm in charge.

___ 2. My children know that I "get" who they are and cherish them exactly as is.

___ 3. I question the truthfulness of whatever thought precipitates my upsets, anger, or worry.

___ 4. My children see me happy and smiling.

___ 5. My children hear me say that I'm grateful to be alive.

___ 6. I participate in volunteer experiences with my children.

___ 7. My children are aware of our extended network of close family and friends and of my efforts to stay connected with them on a regular basis.

___ 8. I prepare and mostly eat healthy, nutritious food.

___ 9. My children are aware of my ongoing efforts to continue learning, either by taking classes, attending lectures and workshops, or participating in online learning programs.

___ 10. My children see me enrich my life by attending concerts, theatrical performances, museums, and galleries; and they accompany me from time to time.

___ 11. My children observe me reading often, for pleasure as well as to expand my horizons.

___ 12. My children know they can count on me to be calm and centered, even when they're telling me something I probably won't like hearing.

___ 13. I ask for help when I need it, eat when I'm hungry, and rest when I'm in danger of burning out.

___ 14. When my children are speaking with me, I generally stop what I'm doing, maintain eye contact, and listen with an open mind.

_____ 15. When things don't go the way I'd hoped or planned, my children know that I have faith that things will work out, and they see me looking on the bright side or understanding the life lesson.

_____ 16. Rather than rush things or attempt to fix my children's problems, I help them feel their frustration and sadness, and I help them come through to adaptation.

Scoring

30-48: Keep up the good work!

17- 30: You may want to set the goal of working on one challenging area each week as you commit to making some positive shifts.

0-16: Please consider finding support for your efforts to improve things in your parenting life. I encourage you to sign up for the *Parenting Without Power Struggles* newsletter or teleclasses for ongoing support.

My Parenting Without Power Struggles Intentions

For additional copies visit
http://www.parentingwithoutpowerstruggles.com

The five aspects of my parenting life I most want to improve:

_____

_____

_____

_____

_____

The specific shifts I intend to make this week towards becoming more of the parent I want to be:

_____

_____

_____

_____

_____

_____

_____

_____

_____

_____

_____

_____

_____

_____

_____

_____

_____

_____

Endnotes

Chapter 1: How to Be the Captain of the Ship Through Calm *and* Stormy Seas

Byron Katie, The Work of Byron Katie [online], *http://www.thework.com/thework.asp.* Accessed July 20, 2008.

Chapter 2: Attachment and Connection

1. Bruce Perry, MD, PhD, Senior Fellow of the Child Trauma Academy.
2. M.D Resnick, P.S. Bearman, R.W. Blum, et al. "Protecting Adolescents from Harm: Findings from the National Longitudinal Study on Adolescent Health." *Journal of the American Medical Association,* 278(10), 823-832, 1997.
3. Cate Dooley and Nikki Fedele, "Mothers and Sons: Raising Relational Boys," *JBMTI* papers, 1999.
4. Gordon Neufeld and Gabor Maté, *Hold On to Your Kids: Why Parents Need to Matter More Than Peers,* Ballantine Books, 2006.

Chapter 3: How to Help Your Kids Have Healthy Relationships with the Members of Their Village

1. Anne Manne, Robin Grille, and Kali Wendorf, *Children's Wellbeing Manifesto, http://www.kindredmedia.com.au/downloads/Manifesto2.pdf.* Accessed July 20, 2008.

Chapter 5: Helping Kids Deal with Frustration

1. Gordon Neufeld and Gabor Maté, *Hold On to Your Kids: Why Parents Need to Matter More Than Peers,* Ballantine Books, 2006.
2. Daniel Amen, *Change Your Brain, Change Your Life,* Three Rivers Press, 1999.

Chapter 7: How to Get Kids to Cooperate

1. Jane Fendelman, *Raising Humane Beings,* Phoenix Rising Counseling, Inc., 2001.

Chapter 9: Every Kid's a Genius

1. Howard Gardner, *Intelligence Reframed: Multiple Intelligences for the 21st Century*, Basic Books, 2000.
2. Thom Hartmann, *The Edison Gene: ADHD and the Gift of the Hunter*, Park Street Press, 2003.
3. Information on both studies obtained from Dr. Andrew Weil, *www.drweil.com*.

Chapter 10: How to Help Kids Avoid Depression and Anxiety

1. U.S. Department of Health & Human Services
2. U.S. Department of Health & Human Services
3. Vilayanur S. Ramachandran and Diane Rogers-Ramachandran, "How Blind Are We?" *Scientific American, 2008 Reports Supplement*, 18(2), July 2008.

Chapter 11: Being Present and Mindful, and Unwinding Without Electricity

1. Susanna Visser, M.S., epidemiologist, National Center on Birth Defects and Developmental Disabilities, U.S. Centers for Disease Control and Prevention, Atlanta; David Marks, Ph.D., psychologist, ADHD Center, Mount Sinai Medical Center, New York City; Sept. 2, 2005, *Morbidity and Mortality Weekly*
2. (U.S. Department of Health & Human Services).
3. Carl Honore, *In Praise of Slowness*, Harper San Francisco, 2004.
4. Kathy Juline, "Awakening to Your Life's Purpose," an interview with Eckhart Tolle, author of *The Power of Now*, reprinted from the October 2006 issue of *Science of Mind*, *http://drs1958.gaia.com/blog/2008/3/science_of_mind_intervi ews_2002_and_2006_eckhart_tolle*. Accessed July 20, 2008.
5. *American Journal of Public Health*, August 28, 2004.
6. UCLA Mindful Awareness Research Center, Semel.

Chapter 12: Launching Children Towards a Life of True Happiness

1. Prem Rawat, *www.elanvital.org*
2. Antoine de Saint-Exupéry, *The Little Prince*, Harcourt, Brace

and World, 1943.

Chapter 13: Empowering Kids to Create Their Very Best Life

1. Marianne Williamson, *A Return to Love*, Harper Paperback, 1996.
2. Eckhart Tolle, webcast interview on XM Radio, 2008.

Drawings by Jennings Spangle and Rene Pergomet
Author photo by Dana Fineman

About the Author

Susan Stiffelman is a credentialed teacher, learning specialist, and licensed Marriage and Family therapist based out of Malibu, California, where she lives with her son, Ari, her dog, Rosie, and on most days, a full and grateful heart.

Susan presents *Parenting Without Power Struggles* workshops around the country at schools, parent organizations, and conferences and welcomes invitations. In addition to offering one-on-one counseling, she also makes her parent coaching services available to parents around the world, via telephone sessions.

Susan offers teleclasses and webinars on a regular basis, where those interested in solidifying and applying the ideas in *Parenting Without Power Struggles* can join other like-minded parents in cyberspace for ongoing support.

Susan Stiffelman, MFT
P.O. Box 4246
Malibu, California 90265
(310) 589-7020
www.parentingwithoutpowerstruggles.com
passionateparent@gmail.com

Acknowledgments

The stage is crowded with the cast of characters deserving of thanks for support in birthing this book.

To my clients and newsletter family: I am honored that you have revealed your life to me so intimately. Thank you for the countless things I've learned from being allowed to witness your journeys.

To the phenomenal group of friends/editors who weighed in on this book, cheering me on and giving me feedback: Anna Anawalt, Steve McKeever, Carol Barth, Sheila Spencer, Mitch Ditkoff, Shari Latta, Kay Gabbard, Thom Hartmann, Larry Cohen, Susie Johnson, June Louks, Chris Kammer, Marilyn Mosely, Pamela Ulich, Randee Bieler, Alan and Marcia Roettinger, Julie Wallach, Kathy Gordon, Mary Natwick, Joel and Heidi Roberts, I can hardly thank you enough. Writing is such a lonely enterprise; I could not have done this without your suggestions, insights, and encouragement.

Thank you to the wonderful Christine Bettencourt, whose editing saved the day, and to Elizabeth Lyon, for keeping your finger so lovingly on the pulse of this project.

To Bonnie Solow, my champion disguised as an agent. Thank you for believing in me. And to my extraordinary editor (and friend) at AOL, Susan Avery—where would I be without you?

To my stellar and dearly beloved friends: Your love, humor and good cheer brighten my world and lighten my load: Sally, Stephie, Joycie, Louise, Warren, Jacqui, Jules, Lynnie, Rives, Barbie, Phyllis, Jennifer, Judi, Gwennie, Micah, Karna, Debbie, Ben, Lucy, Wilson, Dani, Teddy and Patty. You are my family, and I love you.

To Casandra and Jenny: I miss you so. Thank you for remaining so strongly in my heart. I pray to do my best in whatever I can do to help you continue loving your children, knowing that you are still guiding them with the fierce mother-love that you had when you were here.

To Wadi, Hans, Daya, and Amar, and your cherished parents: I'm not sure I would have written this book without the

azing experiences I had traveling the world as your teacher so
iy years ago. You helped me realize how joyfully children
_n when they are allowed to be who they uniquely are. Mrs.
Shinglehausen loves you dearly, and I am more grateful to your
parents than I can say for that extraordinary time.

And to my guides, whose wisdom and inspiration
motivated me to write this book: First and foremost, to Prem
Rawat: Thank you for being my teacher and the spokesperson for
my heart, unfailingly reminding me to drink from the well of joy
within and unrelenting in your commitment to help me remember
to make every moment count.

To Reverend Michael Beckwith: My deepest
appreciation for your support and inspiration. To Byron Katie,
Martha Beck, Gordon Neufeld, Marianne Williamson, Eckhart
Tolle, Janet and Chris Attwood, and so many remarkable humans
who have influenced and uplifted my life: I simply say thank you
for sharing your stunning gifts with the world.

Finally, to my parents: Thank you for instilling in me the
passion for learning that has propelled me towards such an
extraordinary life. Dad: I miss you, love you, and am ever grateful
for the countless ways you helped me create the beautiful life I'm
living. And Mom: Thank you for filling my heart with the best of
yours. I love you.

Bonus Material for Readers of
Parenting Without Power Struggles

In many ways, this book is just a beginning. While you now have a resource to help you along your parenting journey, I offer many other ways to supplement what you've learned here to help you stay on track through the day-to-day ups and downs of real life with kids.

Readers can receive free *Parenting Without Power Struggles* audio downloads and updates by visiting the links below for new ideas, resources, workbook exercises and information:

• Free download of interview with Susan Stiffelman talking about the book *Parenting Without Power Struggles* and how to apply its methods in actual, day-to-day situations
Enter password: pwpsinterview

http://www.parentingwithoutpowerstruggles.com/ppbonusmaterial.html

• To subscribe to the free *Parenting Without Power Struggles* newsletter, please visit:
http://www.parentingwithoutpowerstruggles.com

• For information on *Parenting Without Power Struggles* workshops, group phone calls, online classes, supportive materials or private coaching, please visit:
http://www.parentingwithoutpowerstruggles.com

Made in the USA
Lexington, KY
06 August 2011